COWLEY PUBLICATIONS is a ministry of the brothers of the Society of Saint John the Evangelist, a monastic order in the Episcopal Church. Our mission is to provide books and resources for those seeking spiritual and theological formation. COWLEY PUBLICATIONS is committed to developing a new generation of writers and teachers who will encourage people to think and pray in new ways about spirituality, reconciliation, and the future.

ridiculous packaging

or, my long, strange journey
from atheist to Episcopalian,
in two acts

KAREN FAVREAU

Cowley Publications
Cambridge, Massachusetts

Published in the United States of America by Cowley Publications, a division of the Society of Saint John the Evangelist. No portion of this book may be reproduced, stored in or introduced into a retrieval system, or transmitted, in any form or by any means—including photocopying—without the prior written permission of Cowley Publications, except in the case of brief quotations embedded in critical articles and reviews.

Library of Congress Cataloging-in-Publication Data:
Favreau, Karen, 1968–
  Ridiculous packaging, (or, My long, strange journey from atheist to Episcopalian, in two acts) / Karen Favreau.
    p. cm.
  Includes bibliographical references (p.   ).
  ISBN 1-56101-265-3 (pbk. : alk. paper) 1. Favreau, Karen, 1968–
2. Episcopalians–United States–Biography. 3. Anglican converts–United States–Biography. I. Title: My long, strange journey from Atheist to Episcopalian, in two acts. II. Title.
  BX5995.F38A3 2005
  283'.092–dc22

                                2005003660

Scripture quotations are taken from The New Revised Standard Version of the Bible, © 1989, by the Division of Christian Education of the National Council of the Churches of Christ in the United States of America. Used by permission.

Cover design: Gary Ragaglia

This book was printed in the United States of America on acid-free paper.

Cowley Publications
4 Brattle Street
Cambridge, Massachusetts 02138
800-225-1534 • www.cowley.org

For Margo

Well sometimes, life gives us lessons sent
in ridiculous packaging.

— Dar Williams

Table of Contents

Acknowledgments

Thank you Michael Wilt, not only for believing in the book, but for helping me to become a better writer. Thank you Timothy Staveteig for letting me drop your name. Thank you Mom, Dad, and Patti for your ongoing love and support; I never would have made it this far without you. Thank you Margo for playing proofreader, roadie, and partner so well. Thank you Cowley Publications for taking a chance on me. And thank you Wendy, Elaine K., Cheri & Mark, Marcia & Rob, Barbara, Bob C., Julie, John & Jon, and all the other St. Andrew's angels who welcomed me with open arms; what an amazing community I've found.

Introduction

As Jesus was walking beside the Sea of Galilee,
he saw two brothers, Simon called Peter and his
brother Andrew. They were casting a net into the
lake, for they were fishermen. "Come, follow me,"
Jesus said, "and I will make you fishers of men."
At once they left their nets and followed him.
(Matthew 4:18–20)

That's it? No questions, fears or

regrets? Considering the fact that many of us experience
tremendous angst at the coffee house when choosing
between "Columbian Bold" and "House Blend," I'm amazed
that Peter and Andrew were able to pack it all in so quickly.
Did they experience a pang of remorse over the fact that
they'd just spent mucho denarii on brand-new fishing nets?
Did one of them have a sweetheart in Capernaum who
might not look kindly upon the act of abandoning a secure
job with benefits to follow a radical guru who challenged
the status quo? Did they wrestle with doubt?

I wish I could claim that I too embraced the Divine without a second's hesitation. Instead, I found myself confused
and overwhelmed. It all happened after I'd fallen to my
knees in a moment of desperation, praying for the first time
since I'd been about thirteen. Granted, I'd invoked God's
name a number of times in my twenties while making
drunken plea bargains such as "God, if you just let me make
it home without vomiting, I promise to never drink those
purple things with the vodka and pineapple chunks again,"
but I wouldn't exactly call such conversations meaningful.

Aside from being sober, what made this instance different was that God answered, and it scared the Hell out of me. I'm pretty sure that this was not the first time God spoke to me, slapped me upside the head, grabbed me by the lapels, or shouted in my ear, but I'd always been much too angry, busy, scared, or buzzed to notice.

So why did I notice God this time around?

This book is an attempt to make sense of my spiritual awakening, as well as what it means "to be a Christian." It is a therapeutic exercise in deciphering why a cynical, thirty-three-year-old atheist would open her heart and accept God's love after having spent an entire lifetime running away from him.

Transformation is a beautiful thing. Scary, yes, and a bit messy at times, but beautiful nonetheless. I'm sure that some of my artsy friends will be embarrassed by my very public embrace of a religion that is not as cool as Buddhism or the Kabbalah that Madonna practices, and I can sympathize with them. After all, hearing a friend tell you that he or she has just "found God" can be as unsettling as hearing a loved one utter "I've started writing poetry." These phrases make us uncomfortable because the poet and the proselytizer are so embarrassingly sincere about what they're willing to share. We squirm because our friends have suddenly changed, speaking in a manner that stands in stark contrast to the reserved and closely guarded ways in which we're used to hearing them communicate.

So get ready to squirm.

The book is divided into two parts: "B.C." chronicles my fall from faith, while "A.D." captures my first frantic year after having regained it. I've chosen to focus on the people, authors, and events that contributed heavily to both my loss of faith and my journey back to God. Since the love interests with whom I've been entangled neither pulled me toward nor pushed me away from the Divine, I have not muddled the narrative flow by lapsing into lascivious details about my sometimes wonderful but mostly tragic romantic life; I'll save those for a future memoir.

As I delve deeper into theology and find myself becoming more comfortable in my Christian faith, I'll probably look back at *Ridiculous Packaging* as being somewhat naïve and quaint. Yet, I feel that it is important to preserve a record of my nascent thoughts, fears, and misconceptions so that I never become complacent. By jotting down the little epiphanies and major disappointments I experienced in that first year, I can relive the amazement I felt upon reading the Gospel of Luke for the first time and reminisce about the sense of gratitude that gripped me as I awkwardly got down on my knees to thank God for the gift of grace.

Episcopalian priest Barbara Brown Taylor writes, "Whether we [Christians] like it or not, every one of us is a full-fledged deputy of God's kingdom. Some of us are better at it than others and some of us do more harm than good, but none of us is excused." I can only hope that, in writing about my own twisted journey, I do more good than harm.

God, help us.

B.C.

1

Losing My Religion

I can't pinpoint the exact moment when I lost my faith. I remember the day upon which I defiantly proclaimed that I would no longer attend church, but can't recall if doing so was the *result* or the *cause* of my foray into atheism. Did I wallow through a murky period of agnosticism first, wringing my hands and pacing back and forth before finally choosing a side? Did I grieve the death of my God, or say "I'm sorry" before handing over the reins to the cynical part of my brain? You'd think that such a monumental occurrence would be forever branded upon my brain so that, upon demand, I could look back and say something like "Yup, December 14, 1984, 8:47 A.M.; that's when I decided that this God stuff was a bunch of hooey."

I clearly recall the details surrounding less important events in my life, such as what I was doing when I learned that Ronald Reagan had been shot, and where I was when I took my last drink. Regarding the former, I was sprawled out on the couch in my Catholic school plaids, thoroughly engrossed in a Bugs Bunny cartoon featuring the red, hairy, tennis shoe-clad monster when a "We interrupt this program" message flashed across the screen. I proceeded to run around the house shouting "the President's been shot!" like a manic town crier.

Regarding the latter, it was March 27, 1997, open mike night at the now defunct T.J.'s Pub in Greensboro, North Carolina. I'd limited myself to three beers that evening, but, upon returning to my table after a four-song set, found a bottle of Heineken waiting for me. Worried that refusing the beer would constitute a breach of etiquette, I thanked the friend who'd bought it, drained the bottle, drove home drunk and woke up the next morning feeling as though my head were filled with sand and cigarette butts. I rubbed my temples, proclaimed "That's it" and haven't had a drink since.

Yet the events surrounding the day upon which I officially turned my back on the faith of my childhood are nowhere to be found. Nor can I remember the moment in which it first dawned on me that someday we all will die. I can't recall the date and time in which my youthful exuberance was crushed or where I was when Michael Jackson crossed that thin line between merely eccentric and really, really creepy.

For many men and women my age, Christianity is something that simply ceased to be interesting as more shiny and colorful distractions made themselves known. Sure, they may still claim to believe in God, but God is far away and unknowable, something that doesn't quite fit into their busy schedules or make for interesting dinner conversation. And then there are the folks who never had any faith with which to begin but did not become bold enough to emancipate themselves from the religious wishes of their parents until entering adolescence.

But I *did* have faith; my entire childhood was steeped in it. I dreamed of martyrdom, could recite the entire Catholic Mass by heart, and prayed for the desperate souls in Purgatory, my skinny knees digging into carpet, my hands clenched so tight that I thought they'd go numb. How did it just stop? How did God go from being the center of my universe to nothing but an archaic and downright dangerous illusion?

In the same way that an "overnight success" spends a lifetime preparing for his or her first hit single, the convert does not simply wake up one morning spouting scripture. Rather, conversion is a process. The flash of white light is not an end unto itself but merely a dramatic wake-up call.

Likewise, one does not simply roll out of bed and decide that God does not exist. Losing one's religion, much like gaining it, is also a process. In my case, I believe that the process commenced with the onset of an abdominal disorder that reared its ugly head when I was twelve years old.

At the time, I was a student at Our Lady of the Holy Rosary School, a strict Catholic K-through-12 that my parents attended back when corporal punishment was in vogue. Once run entirely by French-Canadian nuns, lay teachers now held most of the positions. The remaining nuns who had not flown the coop after Vatican II were well past retirement age but hung on out of a stalwart sense of duty; after all, sentences needed to be diagrammed, souls had to be saved, and French verbs waited patiently for conjugation. We were taught to speak proper English by nuns who said things like "Dat dere is not correct grammar," but I respected their authority nonetheless and tried my hardest not to rock the boat.

As I think back to the women in the stiff black habits who dragged themselves into work each day, it saddens me that nuns have become mere caricatures and punch lines in popular culture. The women who taught me in my youth were just as complex and multifaceted as anyone else, privy to their own dreams, desires, and disappointments. Had some of them joined the ranks solely out of family obligation or as a way to avoid the role of wife and mother? Did they get lonely? Did some of the women dream about becoming priests, a role still denied the brightest, most dynamic women in the Catholic Church? Perhaps I too would have entered the convent had I come of age in the 1950s.

I called Gardner, Massachusetts, home. The city's 20,000-odd residents were predominately Catholic and of French-Canadian, Irish, or Polish descent. In the same way that many public school teachers in North Carolina will not assign homework on Wednesday nights to accommodate the Baptists, the public schools in Gardner served fish every Friday in honor of its religious majority.

I bounced between two Catholic churches in my youth, warmly embracing the yin and yang of God's two houses.

Our Lady of the Holy Rosary, the "French church" that was connected to my school, fascinated me. It was imposing and cathedral-like, always smelling of incense and furniture polish. The light from its stained glass windows rained down upon us in blue and red swaths, while heavy-haloed saints gazed at the parishioners from their lofty pedestals. I found myself holding my breath whenever I pushed open the tall, wooden doors. Holy Spirit Parish, the decidedly modern non-ethnic parish to which my family and I belonged, was less somber. In fact, the blond-brick church sported thick, red carpeting that would have fit in nicely at a bordello.

Yes, there were Lutheran, Congregational, Baptist, and Episcopalian churches in our town, but they were irrelevant to my family, not even worth discussing or differentiating. Those were the places where the Others worshiped, and the Others were all the same.

I looked forward to Mass every week and sacrificed Archie comic books and Nestlé Crunch bars for Lent. I wasn't familiar enough with the Old Testament to view God as an angry, vindictive entity, so I imagined him as a loving Creator who took care of his children. However, when I woke up one day in 1980 with a pain in my abdomen that I can only describe as that of a flaming chainsaw slicing through nerve endings, the events that unfolded over the next twelve months caused me to question the "loving" part on God's resume.

After Tums and hot tea failed to quell the pain, I was rushed to the local hospital, where I underwent emergency surgery to correct an intestinal blockage. In the process, the doctors yanked out a gangrenous ovary that had been choked by my wayward intestines. I spent the following week on the children's ward hooked up to tubes while surrounded by comic books, Major League Baseball magazines, and a battered copy of Robin Cook's *Coma,* a reading selection that worried the nurses.

I returned home only to discover that Gardner's finest did not succeed in correcting the blockage; the flaming chainsaw sensation hit me again and again. I'd be sent back to the

Ridiculous Packaging

hospital, where, upon arrival, a tube would be snaked into my stomach via my nose to suck out the pea-soup backwash in my gut. After a few days of bland food and potent painkillers, I'd return home. The nuns and students prayed for my speedy recovery, the redundant Hail Marys flowing from the tinny intercom speakers each morning.

I eventually wound up at Massachusetts General Hospital in Boston. During a third and final operation, my colon was shifted to one side of my abdomen, while my small intestines were anchored to the other. The surgeon widened a defective portion of my duodenum and removed the vast web of scar tissue that had wrapped around my organs. When all was said and done, my abdomen resembled a map of the New York City subway system as drawn by an angry toddler with a pink crayon.

0 0 0

Unlike Patti, my more effusive and outspoken older sister, I'd come to embrace the "honey vs. vinegar" maxim at an early age. Shouting and fussing weren't effective strategies for getting the attention of parents and teachers; in fact, doing so just made them close up their ears all the more. Calm seas brought these people joy, and I tried my best to avoid upsetting anyone. Thus, I did not complain during my trials and suffered stolidly like the saints, who never lost their composure while being stoned, sliced, and stomped by heathens.

One day, while perusing the pages of a Richie Rich comic book, a nurse commented that she'd never seen anybody look so serious while reading cartoons.

I did not allow myself to cry as I pondered whether or not I would be able to play kickball or basketball ever again. Despite my scrawniness, and the fact that I was always singled out as the weak link in our sadistic games of Red Rover, I was the self-proclaimed kickball queen of the segregated asphalt schoolyard. I recall walking outside one afternoon with the red gym ball tucked under my arm, fully prepared to pick off my less athletically inclined classmates in the Darwinian debacle known as dodgeball when I sensed a change in the air. My friends were gathered in a circle, and they ignored me as I bounced the ball impatiently in front of them.

"We're too old to play games," Marcelle finally exclaimed with a disgusted sigh from behind her big glasses and feathered hair. "We're going to talk at recess now."

I felt dizzy, as though someone had violated the sacred dodgeball code and chucked the ball at my head. Oh, how ill-prepared I was for the rocky ride into womanhood. I cared not a lick for those Judy Blume novels with their emotional, menstruating characters, and I wanted to shrink and disappear when my mother sat me down with a pamphlet one night to discuss the glorious miracle of making babies. The only members of the opposite sex I found interesting were those identified as Rolling Stones, Beatles or Red Sox. If my ability to kick, toss, and catch a ball was in any way compromised by my illness, then life itself would not be worth living. But I never shared these fears with anyone.

I maintained my stoic façade while being poked and prodded by residents and interns who, clipboards in hand, stared at me as if I were a dissected frog in a pan while referring to me as "the patient." On the few occasions in which I did betray my emotions, my mother suggested that I offer up my suffering to Jesus and the souls in Purgatory. Unfortunately, as a thirteen-year-old kid, I didn't understand the concept. All I knew was that I'd upheld my end of the bargain with God, and that God didn't appear to be carrying his load.

How I wish someone had explained to me that God is sometimes silent, but never absent.

When I arrived home for an extended recovery period, my family and I did not discuss the enormity of what I had endured. This is not because my parents were cruel or negligent. They'd driven the sixty-plus miles to the hospital in Boston every day to be with me, my father holding my hand and whispering "If I could, I'd take your place on that bed in a minute" into my ear. No, we simply lived in an era in which the term "post-traumatic stress disorder" hadn't worked its way into the lexicon. Oprah was not there urging us to get real, and therapy was still viewed as a last resort for crazy, dangerous individuals who did not participate in the Catholic sacrament of Reconciliation. Life went on. Much as

I'd pretended to believe in Santa Claus as a kid to appease my folks, the act of offering up my pain to Jesus was nothing but a shallow, calculated gesture.

I slowly became numb.

I cannot access the emotions I felt during this period, but I do recall disparate, seemingly pointless details regarding my stay at Massachusetts General. For example, my favorite nurse, who wore too much blue eye shadow, was named Ellen. One of the male interns wore clogs, which struck me as peculiar. A boy whose name I never learned cruised around the ward in a wheelchair while blasting Pat Benatar songs from the boombox on his lap. The art therapist dragged a giant pumpkin into the lounge for Halloween, and those of us on the ward carved it, salted the seeds and baked them. Because my intestines weren't quite ready for nuts, seeds, or other sharp objects, I couldn't partake in the feast.

One of my roommates, a redhead cocooned in a full body cast, wore funky prism glasses in order to watch the television set bracketed to the ceiling while lying flat on her back. After a young man from her school visited, she cracked to the nurse, "Good, he's gone . . . now I can fart." Her ability to joke with the staff appalled me; how dare she laugh and show emotion in such a God-forsaken place?

When I returned home from my three-week stay in Boston, I devoured books on human biology, copiously replicating the illustrations in *Gray's Anatomy* with my markers and colored pencils. Much like the interns, I began to view myself as a frog in a pan. My damaged organs became burnt sienna and orange-red doodles on a sketchpad, my body nothing but poorly constructed luggage.

With a bit of "Stockholm Syndrome" flourish, I became overly grateful to the men and women who had fixed my wayward intestines, despite the physical torment I'd endured. I drew an elaborate operating room scene consisting of anesthesia tanks, computers, a team of scrub-covered doctors, and a pale girl sprawled out on a table; I sent it to the surgeon extraordinaire who had repaired my digestive tract. I bought an "I ♥ Mass General" pin during a follow-up visit and proudly secured it to my brown corduroy pocketbook. I declared that I wanted to be an anesthesiologist when I grew up, though my career goals would change drastically upon receiving a C-minus in high school chemistry. Until then, I dreamed about fixing broken people.

Occasionally, when I smell a particular industrial-strength cleanser, or taste something bitter in the back of my throat, I'll experience a flashback.

*   *   *

When I was no longer hunched over from my incisions, my father took me to the convenience store each day to play Space Invaders and Asteroids. Our visits were carefully timed so as to avoid the scary burnout kids in their jean jackets and Black Sabbath t-shirts who monopolized the video games. When not shooting at virtual aliens, I played a Beatles "greatest hits" album over and over until I knew each word by heart. I "Paul is dead" clues on the covers of *Abbey Road* and *Sergeant Pepper,* learned reams and reams of useless Fab Four trivia and taped Xeroxed photos of Paul and George on my bedroom wall. I was especially fascinated by the Beatles' drug experimentation, curious as to what had inspired John to compose the seemingly nonsensical lyrics to "Lucy in the Sky with Diamonds."

During a follow-up visit to Mass General, the surgeon asked me if I had any questions. I cleared my throat and asked meekly, "Will I be able to have children?" The question sounded strange coming from my lips, as if I were reading a poorly written movie script; I might as well have inquired if I'd be able to continue fighting crime or singing opera competitively. Yet, I assumed that any normal girl my age would want to know if her ability to procreate had been compromised, and that, for the sake of everyone in the room, I should pose the question.

"Yes, you can have babies."

Everybody nodded happily.

———

Numbness unto itself isn't a state of mind that I would recommend to friends, but it served a lifesaving purpose at the time. In a nutshell, it warded off a full-blown mental breakdown. But, like a faulty Internet filter, it kept the bad stuff in and the good stuff out. I no longer experienced highs or lows, and, as I prepared for my first day as a freshman at Gardner High School, I didn't feel a thing.

I waited at the bus stop in my ill-fitting J. C. Penney jeans and thin-striped oxford, trying hard to look preppie, but failing miserably. I was one of many Catholic school geeks who'd be infiltrating the incestuous public school gene pool, a "South Gardnerite" who didn't have a clue as to who was popular and who should be avoided at all costs. Maybe I'd be one of the people to avoid.

I sleepwalked through the first year. I bonded with a small band of likable misfits, played basketball and softball with the good kids, got A's and B's, and fended off potential bullies by poking fun at myself before anyone else got around to it. But when the cold, distant, sleepwalk-state to which I'd become accustomed began to melt beneath the heat of rampaging hormones, the vicious onslaught of new feelings and painful crushes scared the Bejeezus out of me.

I attempted to lose myself in David Bowie cassettes, Kurt Vonnegut novels, and British New Wave magazines. I lived vicariously through the tell-all rock star biographies I devoured, my self-destructive thoughts emboldened by sordid retellings of the escapades of Keith Richards, Brian Jones, and Jim Morrison. I no longer engaged in meaningful conversations with my parents, choosing instead to lock myself in my room for hours, responding to them only in annoyed grunts. I became Darlene from the sitcom *Roseanne,* sans the cutting wit.

When the carefully selected props I'd assembled could no longer dull those scattershot emotions that clothesline us during adolescence, I turned to alcohol.

My first buzz arrived courtesy of a bottle of Tequila stolen from somebody's older brother's secret stash. Despite the fact that the liquor burned my esophagus and muddled my thoughts, it was love at first sight, and the start of a very unbeautiful relationship. Alcohol granted me the ability to turn numbness on and off at will. I was effusive when I drank, and I understood immediately why rock stars loved the stuff. If I stayed sober on any given Saturday evening, it was simply because I couldn't persuade anyone to illegally purchase a bottle of Peppermint Schnapps or Boone's Farm wine for me.

It would be two or three more years before I discovered that most wine bottles come with a cork rather than a twist-off cap.

But I digress . . .

I never got grounded for my weekend debauchery, an amazing feat that I attribute to my own savvy and my parents' elaborate denial. Perhaps it had something to do with the fact that, when I was just a baby, a visiting priest walked up to my mother as she held me, gazed into my squished, pink face, and proclaimed "this is a special child" before exiting the room. Maybe he said this to all of the Catholic moms he ran into, but mine took his words to heart. As a result, I got away with murder. Certainly a child who'd been deemed "special" by a man of the cloth wouldn't be out getting wasted week after week. And if I was up to no-good, then it was surely just a phase, something to kill time before running off to win a Nobel Prize.

When I grew tired of stealing beer and begging for Boone's Farm, I hooked up with a twenty-one-year-old boyfriend named Jay, who was old enough to buy booze legally. I can't remember what we talked about while cruising to the liquor store in his beloved baby-blue Bel Air sedan, but I do remember feeling desperately lonely in Jay's presence.

As the beer flowed and my faith waned, I began to remove all vestiges of Christianity from my bedroom. The picture of Jesus was replaced by an Ozzy Osborne poster; after all, the Oz Man had never let me down. The saint figurines, prayer beads, and the big white Bible I'd won in a Holy Rosary poster contest were relegated to the back of the closet. I allowed the statue of the Virgin Mary to remain only because, after placing a small doll's fedora on her head, she looked remarkably like Boy George.

Since we lived directly across the street from Holy Spirit Church, the only way I could get out of attending Mass on Sunday mornings was to pretend I'd overslept. Unable to keep up the charade for more than a few weeks, I unapologetically announced that I would no longer attend church. My mother called me a "heathen," but, in the same way that we did not discuss the emotional impact of my surgeries, we didn't talk about the fact that I was drifting away from God. Not counting the odd funeral or wedding service, it would be seventeen years before I darkened the door of a church again.

2

Licking the Earth

As a child I loved the high

drama of Catholicism. I devoured books about the colorful
and often violent lives of the saints and found myself inex-
plicably drawn to the martyrs. There was St. Lawrence, for
example, who'd been roasted alive, and St. Catherine, who
had died upon a cruel contraption of wheels and blades.
They bore their suffering with grace and stoicism, and their
allegiance to the One True Church never wavered. In fact, it
is said that Lawrence joked "I'm done on one side, won't you
turn me over?" while he lay on the grill, his flesh falling off
in chunks, his tormentors stunned.

Unbeknownst to my friends and family, I fantasized
about a Soviet invasion in which American Christians
would be forced to pledge allegiance to the Godless system
of Communism. I envisioned myself kneeling bravely before
a stone-faced Russian soldier, the barrel of his rifle pressed
against my head, my hands steepled in prayer.

"Are you, or have you ever been, a Christian?" he would
growl, to which I would proudly proclaim "Yes, yes, I am"
before swiftly joining the ranks of the martyrs.

When not fantasizing about canonization, I assisted in
saving "pagan babies" from a lifetime in Limbo. When my
classmates and I gathered enough milk money and pocket
change to hit the ten-dollar mark, a bloated, third-world
child would be baptized in the name of Jesus Christ. Saving

a soul was exciting unto itself, but the *real* selling point of the endeavor was that we got to name the kid. I can't help but wonder if there's a whole generation of twenty-something Ethiopians out there with names like Farrah, Vinnie, and The Fonz.

Immediately after confessing my iniquities to a priest, I prayed that a car would strike me dead on the way home; this way, my spotless soul would be guaranteed a seat on the express train to Heaven. Not that nine-year-olds were capable of committing sins so heinous as to deny them entry into the pearly gates, mind you, but I clearly had a flair for the dramatic. And the morbid. How much more exciting life would have been had my physical suffering been the result of bloodthirsty communists or pagan rain forest dwellers as opposed to a congenital digestive-tract disorder.

Before illness challenged my faith in God, Catholicism was inextricably woven into my thoughts, words, and deeds. I can still picture myself telling the little girl beside me in third grade that, according to my Mom, the peace sign she'd drawn was a "twisted cross," a sign of the devil. I remember being told by the nuns that *Jesus Christ Superstar* was sacrilegious, that KISS stood for "Kids in the Sources of Satan," and that notorious atheist Madalyn Murray O'Hair was some sort of newfangled Anti-Christ for kicking prayer out of the public schools. Sometimes, it felt as if the world were divided into "Us vs. Them."

Despite the fact that Franco-Americans are the second largest ethnic group in Massachusetts (the Irish being first), most Bay State residents would be at a loss if asked "When you hear the term *French-Canadian,* what comes to mind?" We simply haven't done a very good job at spinning charming or tragic tales à la *My Big Fat Greek Wedding* or *Angela's Ashes.* And while you can't swing a hockey stick without hitting an Italian restaurant, Jewish comedian, or best-selling Irish author, Franco-Americans have never worried much about cornering the market on food, literature, or culture. Unless, that is, you count Celine Dion among the latter.

Franco-Americans didn't hit the United States in a massive flood like the Irish or Swedes; rather, they began trickling in sometime after 1850 to work in the textile plants, paper mills, and furniture factories. Because they assimilated easily, they never really drifted toward identity politics or mobilized along ethnic lines; hence, the lack of a clear, Franco-American identity. Yet, if there's one thing that unites us displaced Canucks, it's the Catholic faith. In New England alone, my forefathers and mothers founded more than 300 churches and 200 parochial schools.

If I were to list some characteristics of my own Franco-American clan, the adjectives *hard-working, reserved,* and *devout* would easily make the top three.

My mother's hard-working, reserved, and devout parents bid adieu to New Brunswick in the early part of the twentieth century in search of meaningful employment. Pepere LeBlanc found it in the bustling factories of Gardner, Massachusetts, where he worked until retirement. While Gardner still sports a good many showrooms, the furniture factories have migrated south. Some of the abandoned buildings have been converted into apartments, while others remain intact, albeit boarded up, serving as brick-and-mortar gravestones in a city that continues to mourn the loss of its industrial base.

Gardner's freakish twelve-foot-high wooden chair still stands, however, despite the fact that its *Guinness Book of World Records* title was usurped by a taller piece of furniture in Thomasville, North Carolina. Perhaps my hometown will one day save face by constructing a disproportionately sized end table.

But I digress . . .

The LeBlancs' first language was French ("gutter French" my mother called it, a dialect comparable to English with a Brooklyn accent), and the language barrier made it difficult to communicate easily with them. Yet my sister Patti and I knew implicitly that they loved us. Memere showered us with homemade bread and bear hugs, and Pepere gave us shiny quarters and challenged us to races, until his arthritic knees betrayed him. They were no-nonsense folks who said the rosary each day, tithed ten percent of their modest income to the church, and were unimpressed by pretense or drama.

I rushed into their house one afternoon, shouting frantically about the giant garden snake Patti and I had encountered in the driveway. Memere rose from the sewing table, stepped outside, grabbed a rock, and smashed its head. Wordlessly, she turned around and went back inside. One night, while watching with Pepere a made-for-TV movie based on Old Testament stories, I asked, "Is that what really happened?" to which he replied, "I don't know. I wasn't there."

My mother was the youngest of seven. She worked all through high school, eventually buying her own car and paying her way through college. She earned a B.A. and a Master's degree in English from Fitchburg State College; somewhere in the mix, she entered the order of the Sisters of the Presentation of Mary, where she served as a novice. My mother left the convent before taking her final vows.

My father was "the responsible one" in the Favreau family. Before the advent of child labor laws, he cleaned chicken cages and set up pins manually at the local bowling alley while just a boy. As a teenager, he worked eighty-hour weeks at Favreau's Gas Station, the family business that my grandfather eventually sold right out from under him. Had he grown up under different circumstances and in a different era, I am sure that my father could have become an engineer, history professor, or architect. But Dad was forced to drop out of high school in order to work at his father's gas station. He later obtained his GED and secured a job as a mechanic at a utilities company.

My father has always been a bottomless font of nervous energy, a miasma of nervous tics and twitching fingers. Before trading in his motorcycle for marriage vows, Dad was known to occasionally hop onto his Harley and drive to Florida just for the hell of it, returning in time for his Monday morning shift at the station. He is forever "tinkering" in the basement, creating model airplanes and boats and fussing with this or that while AM radio drones on in the background.

While I suppose I've inherited my unquenchable restlessness from my father, I've always been terrified of motorcycles.

❀ ❀ ❀

The Gardner of my youth was unspectacular. Factories and triple-decker apartments shared the hilly landscape with liquor stores, brick schoolhouses, and mom-and-pop businesses that have since been replaced by the chains. Two of the downtown district's more popular destinations included a candlepin bowling alley and a one-screen movie theater in which I witnessed such cinematic classic as *Porky's II* and *Footloose.* On weekends, teenagers hung out in the parking lot of McDonald's or cruised up and down the main drag, going nowhere but driving way too fast to get there.

The popular kids got drunk behind the high school in a scraggly patch of woods called the Bayou. After a surprise police raid in which a number of my classmates got snagged for underage drinking, those of us who never made the guest list couldn't help but smile. In the summers, we basked in the sun at the Polish American Country Club, a fancy name for what was essentially a pond, a stretch of sand, and a hot dog stand. Outdoor concerts featuring washed-up rock bands were held here each summer, and I had the pleasure of watching both Steppenwolf and the Guess Who perform during my senior year. After the latter concert, I was disappointed to learn that the only original member of the band had been the bass player; I bought their *Greatest Hits* anyway.

I can count the total number of African-American classmates with whom I'd graduated on two fingers, and I would not make any Jewish friends until I got to college; perhaps this is why I didn't catch most of the punch lines in *Annie Hall* and *Hannah and Her Sisters* as a teenager. A group of Laotian "boat people" and a few Hispanics lived in a low-cost housing project called Olde English Village, Gardner's own version of a ghetto. When a friend's bicycle was stolen from outside a department store one summer, many folks jumped to the conclusion that the crime was committed by Puerto Ricans from "The Village."

I stumbled upon a novel by Bill Morrissey called *Edson* some years ago and couldn't help but smile as I read the following passage about the economically depressed New England mill town in which the story unfolds:

> At the town line his headlights flashed on a statue of the Blessed Virgin set up on a knoll between the road and the Edson River. Keeping her back to the town, she greeted each oncoming car with her palms open at her sides, her shoulders hiked in a permanent shrug as if to say, "Welcome to Edson. It's not my fault."

"My God," I thought, "he's been to Gardner!"

Unlike the glassy-eyed stoners who camped out on "the Path," their school binders covered in black marker renditions of marijuana leafs, the Van Halen logo and misspelled Doors lyrics, my pot consumption was done surreptitiously. I played sports, but wasn't good enough to be labeled as a jock. I was an artist who worried too much about what people thought of me to ever dye my hair blue or acquire an entirely black wardrobe. And I was an honors student who received A's in A.P. history and English and C's in algebra and chemistry. I was a burnout, a brain, an artist, and an athlete, all of the *Breakfast Club* characters, sans Molly Ringwald, rolled up into one amorphous mess of an identity crisis.

And, despite having lost my virginity to a nineteen-year-old army private when I was only sixteen, I did not belong to that tribe of big-haired "bad girls" who ditched pep rallies, smoked in the girls' room, and dated from outside the pool of pimply-faced boys at our high school. Unlike them, I still participated in extracurricular activities and clamored for acceptance from the popular kids. For me, boys were just a distraction and not something upon which to base my reputation.

I hung out with other blue-collar kids, our expectations low, our eyes firmly set on the horizon. Jen, Mo, and I promised one another that we would not end up like those Gardner gals who'd married their high school sweethearts, squeezed out a kid within a year, and wound up working at the local pizza joint. And we most certainly weren't going to be anything like our parents.

The three of us ended up at the University of Massachusetts in Amherst. This culturally rich, ultra-liberal, and socially diverse town lay only forty-five minutes down the road from Gardner, but it seemed more like forty-five hours. While much of the student body there was made up of factory-town folks like ourselves, we also came face to face with students who were not working-class or Catholic. I met savvy, street-smart students from Boston and New York City, wealthy kids from Newton and Lexington, and exotic exchange-students from Africa and the Caribbean. Despite my burning desire to get out of straight, homogeneous Gardner, I cried every night for two weeks from the culture shock.

I remember leaning out my window on a crisp, autumn day, my gaze fixed upon the patchwork-quilt campus that stretched out like a small country before me. Atop that steep hill in Van Meter Dormitory, I felt very small and very scared. The prospect of living in a dorm with a hundred or so fellow freshmen was both thrilling and terrifying; part of me wanted to swallow the campus whole, while the other wanted nothing more than to leap from that high window and plunge to my death.

How would I single out friends from the massive throng that called the University of Massachusetts home? How would I forge an identity from which I could glean comfort and security? By the end of the first week, I'd figured it out. No, my quest for community and identity did not involve joining the staff of the campus newspaper, attending events at the Newman Center, or diving headfirst into campus politics. Rather, it involved drinking.

Like many college freshmen, I had already developed an unhealthy dependence on alcohol by the time I entered the hallowed halls of higher learning. And it wouldn't take long for me to find other students who shared my passion. Despite the fact that my friends and I were all under twenty-one, we were infused with a sense of entitlement regarding the right to get sloppy drunk three or four nights a week.

We drank and smoked pot from Thursday night ("Thirsty Thursday") through the wee hours of Sunday morning while the resident assistants turned a blind eye to our activities. We experimented with LSD and mushrooms. We learned to love the Grateful Dead, or at least to *pretend* to love those incoherent lyrics, live bootleg tapes, and thirty-minute-long guitar solos that noodled off into oblivion. We wore tie-dye t-shirts and fancied ourselves counterculture rebels, despite the fact that pot smoking and leftist politics were the norm on campus. We criticized Reagan a lot but did nothing constructive to change society for the better. As the late Phil Ochs sang in "Small Circle of Friends," his scathing ode to apathy: "Demonstrations are a drag, besides, we're much too high."

During my junior year, I was involved in a frightening scenario that should've scared me straight, or at least caused me to engage in a bit of reflection. My friend Ellen and I had traipsed across campus one night to visit our friend Jack, a self-absorbed pothead and drug dealer who spoke in a soothing Louisiana drawl. He wasn't the savviest dealer on campus, however, as he carried huge stashes of pot and LSD in his omnipresent army bag at all times, conducting deals right out on the Campus Center concourse. Oh, the pointless cockiness of youth.

We found him in his room surrounded by pounds of pot that he proceeded to weigh and roll neatly into plastic baggies; his knowledge of the metric system was impressive. Ellen and I joined two other acquaintances who'd been hanging out, and we wiled away the evening listening to music, smoking, reading comic books, and chatting with Jack while he continued to divvy up his stash. Then there was a knock on the door, and our host welcomed two men we'd never met into the cramped, cinderblock-walled room. Within seconds, the strange men whipped out pistols, shouted "Police," and ordered us to kneel on the floor with our hands on our heads. I remember staring at them and smiling stupidly, because the events unfolding before me were so absurd and so beyond recognition.

After a second "request," I got on the floor.

Jack was dragged from the room, and the rest of us were instructed to sit on the bed. The undercover policemen informed us that we were all guilty of possession.

"But we're not dealers," Ellen stated. "How can we be guilty of anything?"

"You were surrounded by thousands of dollars of illegal drugs, and you made no effort to leave or call the authorities. You're guilty of possession."

He had a point.

The policemen proceeded to grill us about the people with whom Jack associated. They inquired about his habits and asked us if we knew where he might have acquired the stash. Since none of us even knew Jack's last name, we weren't able to offer up much information. We were finally excused.

"If we ever see your faces again, you are all in deep trouble," the policemen told us as we exited the dorm room.

I did not thank God for allowing the small blotter of acid in my right front pocket to go unnoticed. I did not thank the generous policemen for their leniency. Nor did I take a long, hard look at the self-destructive activities in which I was engaging, or the questionable company that I was keeping. Instead, I went back to my dorm, rallied together as many people as I could and shared the exciting tale of my encounter with "the pigs." With each retelling, the guns got bigger and the police got meaner; I think I even claimed that one of the cops put his pistol up to my head when I "defiantly" refused to get on the floor.

While the characters and setting had changed, it was "Us vs. Them" all over again.

@ @ @

Somehow, thanks to a flyer taped to a plexi-glass bus stop shelter, I began taking guitar lessons and discovered a passion that did not involve booze or bongs. I'd received no formal musical training in my youth (my Catholic school did not have a marching band), and neither of my parents played an instrument. In fact, there wasn't a great deal of music played in our house while I was growing up, except on those Saturday nights when the family gathered around the TV to watch *The Lawrence Welk Show.* Despite my obsessive love of rock music and the surreptitious air guitar sessions I held in my bedroom, I had never seriously entertained the notion of tackling an instrument.

My twenty-one-year-old, booze-buying ex-boyfriend Jay had played guitar, but we girlfriends had sat idly on the sidelines while he and the boys jammed.

"Damn it, I want to be a rock star too!" I exclaimed as I pulled off the tab, tired of letting the boys have all the fun. I begged my parents to buy me a cheap guitar, and I made the call.

In his Birkenstock sandals, John Lennon glasses, and Marcia Brady hair, Doug Hewitt looked as if he'd stepped off the cover of an Iron Butterfly album. His tapestry-draped studio became an oasis amidst the insecurity, craziness, and confusion that epitomized my first semester. He sang with his eyes closed and his head tossed back, each note a glorious gift; I was much too insecure about my vocal abilities at the time to join in.

Doug's passion for the guitar was infectious, and I became so enamored by my teacher that I practiced every night in an effort to make him proud. I stumbled through "Me and Bobbie McGee," "Mrs. Robinson" and other classic rock tunes over and over until they began to take shape. My hands swelled and my finger tips got numb, but I kept practicing anyway, determined to make up for those lost, empty years that had not included the guitar.

Much as I'd hoped, I met many people through my guitar playing. Unfortunately, they all drank.

With my laziness and indifference regarding church attendance, aided by the leftist political climate at the University, my rejection of God and all things religious turned into flatout atheism. My professors spoke of the Church as nothing more than an oppressive, woman-hating, imperialistic institution and viewed Christianity as one-dimensional, archaic, and antithetical to reason. When a radical feminist organization spray-painted "Dethrone the Male God" on a Catholic church in Amherst one Easter weekend, the campus newspaper editors did not scream out in indignation; in fact, barely *anyone* on campus batted an eye.

Protest rallies such as Young Republican "Straight Pride" events and the Radical Student Union's demand that the University's Minuteman mascot be retired due to his status as a "white male with a gun" were held almost every day. Buildings were occupied, classes were canceled, and creative placards were proffered. The University's vitriolic anti-CIA rally garnered so much national publicity that Amy Carter and Abbie Hoffman even drove into town to help out with the hell-raising.

Aside from the anti-CIA rally, one of the largest and most well attended protests during my four years at UMass did not involve politics at all. Because of Chancellor Duffy's decree that alcohol would no longer be allowed at outdoor concerts, students who couldn't find Canada on a map suddenly found themselves becoming activists. I made a sign that read "Dose Duffy," a retaliatory reference to spiking his beverage with LSD, but was outdone by a group of students who carried a giant, inflatable replica of a Bartles & James wine cooler bottle.

Despite our impassioned pleas and cool props, the ban stood. Some of my friends tried to get around this resolution by burying a keg in the ground the night before an outdoor musical event. As morning unfolded, they'd forgotten where they'd buried the thing and spent the whole afternoon, tap in hand, asking concert-goers if they could peek under their blankets and lawn chairs.

But I digress . . .

Catholicism had once been beyond reproach, but I now took great joy in bashing my rejected faith. My conversations were peppered with references to chauvinism, oppression and, in the midst of a lull, the Spanish Inquisition. My "recovering Catholic" friends and I took potshots at the nuns, who are always easy targets, and we lamented the ways in which Catholicism had contributed to our own repression. But what was it that I was really complaining about?

In all my years as a Catholic parishioner, I'd never once heard a priest condemn homosexuals or speak disparagingly about women from the pulpit. Holy Spirit Church switched to "inclusive language" sometime during my adolescence, as the notion of exclusively using male pronouns proved too un-hip even for the old-time priests. My memories of the Catholic youth group to which I belonged are nothing but warm and fuzzy, and, while my school had been strict, I enjoyed my time there. In fact, I'm quite grateful to have had an entire convent and student body praying for me during my prolonged illness.

I guess I never bothered to think about what "being Catholic" meant to me. Author Patricia Hampl writes that "Catholicism itself came to us as aura, not as dogma," and I couldn't agree more. Yes, I remember some specific dogma regarding topics such as Purgatory and the pope; but it's the exotic scent of the incense, the hushed tones, the contemplation and self-denial, the glass-encased relics of St. Anne's wrist bone at her eponymous basilica in Quebec and the agonized expression on Jesus' face as he hung on the big wooden cross at Holy Rosary Church that I remember, mysterious phenomena that burrowed into my being. I can't articulate the difference between a "venial sin" and a "mortal sin," but the aura remains. Is that what I was rebelling against, the aura that wouldn't go away?

I believe that, on some level, my use of pot and other drugs was an attempt to recreate the rituals I'd experienced in the Church. When my friends and I gathered to get high, we made sure that the lights were low, and that the music on the stereo was appropriate for the sacred task at hand; *Led Zeppelin IV* was always a favorite, with the Grateful Dead's *American Beauty* coming in at a close second. We'd gather the necessary accoutrements (roach clip, rolling papers, maybe a ridiculously tall, purple bong), sit down in a circle and watch reverently as the host lovingly rolled a joint or packed the bong. The pot was then shared in a communal feast, making us an ersatz congregation.

Like the Christian Bible, our holy book was composed of various works from diverse sources: *The Electric Kool-Aid Acid Test;* issues of *High Times; Steal This Book; Fear and Loathing In Las Vegas;* worn out paperbacks on Eastern religions; the *Woodstock* soundtrack. These materials helped us master the correct terminology associated with our lifestyle and gave us a sense of belonging to the countercultural community. We'd sit in awe at the feet of older and wiser stoners as they embellished tales about scoring dope in Amsterdam or outsmarting the cops in San Francisco. We were hungry for knowledge and desperate for something, *anything,* to give our God-free lives meaning and purpose.

Because I no longer adhered to any sort of divine guidelines or moral codes, I was free to "lick the earth," a phrase used by Blaise Pascal to describe St. Augustine's less-than-noble youth. If it felt good, I did it. I believed that unfettered freedom and the complete absence of remorse were blessings, as opposed to the curses I would later discover them to be. But, despite the freedom and non-stop debauchery, I was miserable.

Yes, there were devout Christians on campus, but they tended to keep to themselves. We mocked the Campus Crusade for Christ flyers we encountered and couldn't figure out why some of our party buddies still dragged themselves out of bed on Sunday mornings to attend Mass. We never asked them why, and they never dared offer reasons for fear of being teased. While my acquaintances and I were all lost, we couldn't fathom living our lives any other way. If someone had approached me at this point in my life and predicted that, in fifteen years, I would be a sober, non-smoking vegetarian who attended church every Sunday, I would have laughed in his or her face, called security, or run like hell.

While writing a sociology paper on my trusty electric typewriter one morning, severely hung over, I took a few tokes off a joint with the hope that doing so might clear my head. It did not, and I went to bed. As I lay there, I allowed myself to admit that I might just have a drinking problem. I decided that "drying out" might be fun in a twisted sort of way, and that a few months without booze would help get my head together so that I could start drinking more responsibly.

I kept a journal during this period:

> Day 3: You [referring to myself] worry where to
> get it (alcohol), how to get it, who's gonna get it,
> who you'll drink it with and where you'll drink
> it . . . and you love opening your fridge and see-
> ing it lined with brightly colored cans of beer.
> You fondle one, open it, savor every sip. You're
> somewhere else now and you never want to go
> back cuz where you came from wasn't very
> good . . . It [alcohol] is the focus of all your activi-
> ties. It's where all your money goes. It's gotten
> you in trouble with the law, made you injure
> yourself and made you say things that hurt you
> and others. Yet, your love is so strong that you
> stand by your can like a faithful wife, remember-
> ing the honeymoon days, not the hangovers and
> missed classes and depression.

I remember thinking at the time that the "stand by your can" phrase was particularly inspired, but, hey, I was nine-teen, which is about how old Jewel probably was when she wrote the amateurish poetry that wound up in her book *Nights Without Armor*. There's something to be said for not achieving commercial success in one's youth.

The "injure yourself" line refers to the two times I sprained my leg while I was drunk, and the instance in which I was so impaired that I missed my mouth and smashed my front tooth with a beer bottle; I informed my parents that I'd done so with a bottle of Pepsi, even though I've never really cared for soda.

> Day 4: What if I become BORING? What if I
> become a bore and just want to stay home and
> watch TV on Friday nights?

Of course, I had no idea then that my friends and I *were* incredibly boring. Vomiting profusely, engaging in lengthy, slurred discussions about the relevance of Laverne and Shirley's migration from Milwaukee to Los Angeles, playing drinking games and participating in drama queen antics that nobody remembered the next morning—this was hardly riveting stuff. I probably said things like "Have you ever thought that maybe, right now, we're dreaming, and that our dreams are really reality?" while tripping on mushrooms, though I like to imagine that some of my observations were piquant and less clichéd.

> Day 5: So how can other people think I'm cool if I don't drink? I don't want to look like an uptight nerd. I don't want people to think I'm uptight or religious.

I find the line "I don't want people to think I'm uptight or religious" particularly odd, but I'm not surprised that I wrote it. Of course, since becoming an Episcopalian, I've discovered that *alcohol* and *religious* are not mutually exclusive terms.

Despite my initial fears and struggles, I managed to stay sober for nine months. Unfortunately, I fell off the wagon with a resounding thud after just three or four days in Denmark, a country that, in addition to producing beer so potent that it can't be sold legally in the United States, does not believe in enforcing a minimum drinking age.

I was growing tired of my identity as a pseudo-hippie. Thus, after having completed an introductory course on history's most influential social theorists, I decided that I was a Marxist; Durkheim and Weber just weren't as sexy. I borrowed *Das Kapital* from the library, reading just enough convoluted paragraphs to rattle off the occasional deep-sounding riff. I even bought a red t-shirt featuring Karl Marx standing in solidarity beside Groucho, Chico, and Harpo; the accompanying caption read "Sure, I'm a Marxist."

My "radicalization" was in no way unique. I was just one in a long line of kids who, upon returning home for Christmas vacation, found themselves arguing vehemently about politics with Dad. I spoke of liberating the oppressed masses but didn't want to actually mingle with them; the proletariat looked more appealing on paper than in person. When I parroted snippets from the sociology lectures I attended, my knowledge of United States and world history wasn't thorough enough to place my comments in any meaningful context. But I shot my mouth off anyway.

After a particularly inspiring sociology lecture on the Scandinavian welfare state, I signed up for a semester at the University of Copenhagen. Because I was not a fan of children at the time, I requested a "non-traditional" host family and ended up with Kurt and Klaus. The two bachelors shared a funky apartment in the center of town, and I quickly became the envy of all those classmates who'd landed in the suburbs with surrogate moms and dads.

The country of Kierkegaard, Hans Christian Andersen, Carlsburg beer, and Legos was a wonderfully strange and progressive place, the perfect stomping ground for an inquisitive sociology major. Health care and education were viewed as "rights" and thus offered freely to the citizenry. Same-sex marriage was legal long before Massachusetts caught on. Bicycles were the preferred mode of transportation, and the train system was flawless. Homelessness was not abundant, and violence was almost a non-issue; in fact, the prison we visited for a criminology class looked very much like a community college, and Copenhagen's red light district seemed surprisingly quaint. The country did, however, have a problem with rampant bicycle theft.

Because I had no interest in God, I was not saddened to hear Danish citizens tell me again and again that "Nobody goes to church in Denmark." At the time, this news became just one more reason to love the country. I was, however, distraught by the realization that Denmark ranks frighteningly high among Western nations for both suicide and alcoholism rates. It was not uncommon to observe a peer stumbling into class an hour late while lamenting "Sorry, but somebody jumped in front of my train again."

I wrestled with the question "How can people be so unhappy in such a wonderful country?" while smoking highly taxed cigarettes and drinking Tubørg beer in Kurt and Klaus's apartment. Danish society was progressive and humane, and the country's citizens wanted for nothing. I eventually attributed the abnormal suicide rate to the rather stoic nature of the Danish people. It never occurred to me that, in addition, the cause could very well involve the fact that "Nobody goes to church in Denmark."

———— ◆ ————

While on a three-day break from my studies at the University of Copenhagen, some classmates and I traveled to East Berlin. Our bags were searched by walking, talking caricatures in jackboots. We exchanged Danish krøner for East German coins that reminded me of the plastic ones used by Patti and me when playing "grocery store" as preschoolers. And we experienced the Berlin wall in all of its notorious, oppressive, deadly splendor, completely oblivious to the fact that it would be demolished one month later.

As we entered the city, everything around us took on a dull, gray sheen. Sad-eyed, broken men and women shuffled down the sidewalks. Buildings that had been bombed in World War II still lay in ruins. We visited three different restaurants before we found one that actually had food in stock. And the beer? It tasted as I imagine oil would taste after sloshing around an engine for years; but I drank it anyway.

My traveling companions and I met a handsome college student who agreed to accompany us as we walked around the city. Upon reaching a park that sported a large statue of Marx and Engels, I ran toward it, shouting "Let's take a picture!" The once-affable student's demeanor changed as he crossed the street and muttered, "I refuse to set foot in that place."

Undaunted by his reaction, I asked a classmate of mine to snap a photo as I put my hand on Karl's massive thigh and thrust an enthusiastic "thumbs up" toward the camera. After my vulgar display, we continued our trek with the poor young man, who knew too well what it meant to live under the thumb of communism.

While my trip to Europe did not bring me closer to God, it did at least shatter my romanticism regarding Marxism. I came to realize that some things look better in theory than they do in action, a golden nugget of wisdom that I would all too quickly misplace when I embraced Libertarianism four years later.

To this day, the only Danish vocabulary word I can remember is *øl*, which means "beer."

3

Spiritual Indolence

After graduating with a much-

coveted, highly marketable B.A. in sociology in the summer of 1990, I drifted back to my always-generous parents' house. I landed a job filing microfiche at a company that made turbine engines, but boredom and wanderlust quickly got the best of me. I packed up the car, hit the road, and found myself crashing in New Rochelle, New York, with a college love-interest with whom I'd been carrying on a long-distance romance.

College towns are wonderful, but they do have an insulating effect on their residents. I'd gotten so used to living amongst polite, well-read liberals who listened to folk music, attended poetry readings, and smiled at one another between sips of herbal tea that I was completely caught off guard by the noise, crowds, and downright rudeness I encountered upon moving to the greater New York City area.

I scanned the "Help Wanted" section of the paper each morning and watched my recreational cigarette habit snowball into full-blown addiction. An acquaintance of mine suggested that I apply for a job at a homeless shelter in White Plains that served HIV-positive, drug-addicted clients, so I threw my hat into the ring. Even though my knowledge of urban poverty and inner-city drug abuse at the time was limited to what I'd culled from sociology textbooks and

3

Ridiculous Packaging

Good Times reruns, I rose to the occasion and landed myself a job. Perhaps altruism and a lingering desire to "fix broken people" were my reasons for accepting such a challenging gig, though the fact that I wasn't qualified to do anything in particular probably sealed the deal. Or maybe I believed that my own shortcomings wouldn't look quite so bad when compared to those of the homeless.

The shelter had originally been created as a place for HIV-positive men and women to gain some dignity before they died. As new medications were developed, however, the shelter's mission changed to that of providing a safe haven for those who wished to clean up their act so that they could live full lives.

I developed a love/hate relationship with the men and women in the house. On the one hand, I found most of them to be quite charming in a hardscrabble, "hooker-with-a-heart-of-gold" sort of way. Even though many of the male residents had done hard time in the big house, sold drugs, and/or worked as pimps, they were surprisingly chivalrous toward me. If a new resident cursed and used questionable language, the old-timers popped in to say, "Watch it, man, there's a lady in the room!" Some even held the door open for me. The healthier clients and I would play basketball, take in movies, and play cards during my shift, all of us chain-smoking and talking-trash. I even drove the gang to Manhattan in our lumbering thirteen-seat van to catch the *Geraldo* show one afternoon, back in the days before he became a "serious" journalist.

When Halloween rolled around, the somber mood that usually permeated the house gave way to giddiness. With a pile of face paints from CVS, I successfully transformed clients into devils, vampires, various members of KISS, and adorable kitty-cats. My Axl Rose costume proved to be a hit during that first October at the shelter, but, when I dressed up as The Village People's "leather man" the following year, even the most flamboyant drag queens in residence reluctantly admitted that they'd been upstaged.

But I digress . . .

Yes, I developed an affinity for the guys and gals that called the shelter home, but I was angry at the clients for not letting us *fix* them. They skipped Narcotics Anonymous meetings, sneaked drugs into the shelter, and called the meals we served them dog food. Many returned to the streets rather than abide by the few rules that governed the house. Some double-dipped into their welfare benefits and showed up at the shelter with new shoes and leather coats, while my co-workers and I barely made enough to pay our bills. I had no clue as to how one saves a person, but I was angry that they wouldn't even let me try.

❂ ❂ ❂

Considering the fact that I'd felt *small* at the University of Massachusetts, I felt completely invisible each time I drove into Manhattan to cruise the used record stores and comic book shops in the East Village. I was fascinated by the city's grittiness and astounded by the sheer volume of human depravity that surrounded me. But I secretly feared for my safety each time I walked through Tompkins Square Park or caught the subway at night. I purchased a thick black biker jacket and perfected my "Do not even think about approaching me" stare; I got so good at the latter that the squeegee guys on the Henry Hudson Parkway no longer tried to wash my windshield or badger me for money. I also developed an affinity for The Punisher, a DC Comics vigilante who blew big city thugs away with his arsenal of weapons, sans judge and jury.

Because I had little money and even fewer friends, people-watching became a favorite pastime. I'd order a cup of tea from some hole-in-the-wall restaurant, sit at an outdoor table and milk my beverage for hours. I gazed longingly at the punks, club kids, and freaks as they sauntered by, completely comfortable in their own tattooed skin, clearly at home in their element. I envied their devil-may-care attitude and hated the fact that they'd found an identity, while I was still wavering.

On some nights, while cranking the Red Hot Chili Peppers' "Under the Bridge" at full volume, I would drive through the meatpacking district to gawk at the transsexual prostitutes and crack whores. I was Jane Goodall in the concrete jungle, watching, taking notes, and never getting too close while safe in my Dodge K Car, immersed in my own perverse, inner-city safari.

My romantic relationship slowly crumbled, and, out of sheer loneliness, I began to attend Alcoholics Anonymous meetings. Though I knew little about the organization and was not a fan of "groups" in general, I gave it a shot. I thought A.A. would be nothing more than a place where folks could drop by once or twice a week to share their struggles and concerns. Maybe we could all go out for pizza, catch a Yankees game or engage in other "good, clean fun" activities now and then, arm-in-arm as sober allies in a beer-drenched world.

But A.A. turned out to involve a bit more than soda and ball games. I quickly discovered that the program was highly structured and dogmatic. I was told to accept the idea that A.A. is, unto itself, an infallible program, that alcoholism is a disease and that focusing incessantly on one small facet of your life while only hanging out with others who focus incessantly on one small facet of their lives is the best way to stay sober. When I questioned the basics tenets of the program, I learned that I was "in denial."

I also had trouble with that whole "higher power" part. After telling old-timers that I was an atheist, they would smile condescendingly before informing me that I *would* have a spiritual awakening. One woman suggested that I just randomly pick something, anything, as my higher power, such as a chair or a table, until I had this promised awakening. I couldn't quite envision calling out to my sofa in a moment of desperation, but I smiled politely, scared that I'd be labeled "in denial" if I didn't. They also told me that, if I left the safety of the flock, I would start drinking again, and that if I started drinking again I would end up dead, in prison, or institutionalized. They seemed to know a lot about me.

In no way am I insinuating that A.A. is a terrible program that should be eradicated. It has helped countless men and women lay off the booze and rebuild their lives, which is a wonderful thing. No, the biggest problem I have with A.A. and twelve-step programs in general involves the claim that there is one and *only* one way to get and stay sober. A.A. folks tell newcomers straight out that people who "just quit" without the aid of a structured program are "not really sober."

I am a big fan of the Episcopal Church, but I would never suggest that the only proper and effective way for Christians to praise God involves joining the Anglican ranks. No, some people like their worship services to be loud and rowdy, full of "Amens" and "Hallelujahs." Some speak in tongues, while others sit in silence until one of their own is moved by the Spirit. An African-American friend of mine told me that her mother exclaimed, "That thing was as dry as a soda cracker" upon sitting through her first Episcopalian service.

Nor do I think that there is only one way to get sober. Many of us "just quit," which is what smokers used to do before feel-good pacifiers such as nicotine gum and patches came along. Mick Mars, guitarist for Mötley Crüe, shared his own unique method for laying off alcohol in the early days of his sobriety: "Whenever I craved a drink or felt frustrated, I'd just curl up my fingers into a circle as if I were holding a shot glass, yell 'boom', and snap my hand toward my mouth, as if I was hammering a shot of tequila. That was my boom, my therapy. I think it scared a lot of people, but it made me happy. It was also a lot cheaper than rehab."

It's all good.

After being seduced by a trusted A.A. old-timer who had taken way too much of an interest in my life, I stopped going to meetings. As a result, I found myself blessed with a tremendous amount of time on my hands. I signed up for some non-credit night classes at the School of Visual Arts and allowed myself to nurture an innate drawing talent that I'd hidden away for years. It wouldn't be long before my mildly successful career as a freelance cartoonist would take off.

One day, while sketching a moon-faced and rather nondescript model, I thought to myself, "Hey, I could do that!" Granted, I'd always been a modest person who'd never even worn a bikini in public (Mom informed me at a young age that God frowns on bikinis), but something in me craved to be expressed in a big, unusual way. Maybe I was just tired of being "invisible," invisible in the city, invisible in groups, and invisible to my parents, who, regardless of my juvenile delinquent cries for attention, continued to view me as "the good child." Standing buck naked in front of a room full of strangers renders one anything but invisible. So I called various studios and colleges in the area and secured some gigs as an art model.

While this unusual part-time job provided me with extra money and some much needed attention, it also allowed me to become more comfortable in my own skin. I wore the scars on my abdomen like a pink badge of courage. Let's face it, anyone can walk into a tattoo parlor and get a Chinese symbol or the Motorhead logo inked onto his flesh, but surgical scars are *earned,* and are most definitely not for the squeamish. I also discovered an inner grace that I'd never acknowledged. And, because of this newfound appreciation for my body, I quit smoking, a challenging task when working at a homeless shelter in which everyone, staff and clients alike, smoked like fiends.

My restlessness returned, and I reached for the bottle once again. Despite my repeated attempts at seeking out distractions, I felt aimless and empty. With nothing else to fill the void, bitterness and anger started to creep in. I was angry at the folks in A.A. for letting me down. I was angry at the shelter clients for not only being ungrateful, but dying on me as well. I was angry at myself for wasting four years of college. I cursed the ivory-tower, limousine-liberal professors who'd filled my head with the false hopes of Marxism, professors who'd never worked in a homeless shelter or had to buy a biker jacket to feel safe in a cold, overwhelming world.

It was at this point that I stumbled upon the writings of a certain Ayn Rand, the queen of laissez-faire capitalism, rugged individualism, and hardcore atheism. I read and re-read *The Fountainhead,* that classic "architect meets girl, architect rapes girl, architect blows up building" story that continues to win hearts and minds. I highlighted passages on dog-eared pages, convinced that I'd stumbled upon a bottomless font of timeless wisdom.

According to Ms. Rand, altruism is not a noble virtue, but a morally corrupt one. Acts such as sharing one's money with the poor or putting one's best-laid plans on hold to support a sick parent or a needy friend are ultimately destructive to the individual and society as a whole. Yes, in the black-and-white world of her novels, selfish industrialists and fat-cat capitalists are society's ideal men, while union organizers and social workers are perpetuators of perversity. As tortured *Fountainhead* hero and Ayn Rand mouthpiece Howard Roark proclaims in the novel's climactic courtroom scene, "The world is perishing from an orgy of self-sacrificing."

Interestingly enough, while Ayn and my ex-buddy Karl Marx were polar opposites on the political spectrum, they both viewed religion as a terrible and rather frivolous thing. To Karl, it was an opiate that threatened allegiance to the State. To Ayn, a belief in a higher power was a malignancy that threatened the person's status as a rational being.

I ate this stuff up with a spoon.

By way of *The Fountainhead* I became a card-carrying member of the Libertarian Party. I engaged in drunken rants about the decline of Western civilization and made annoying proclamations like, "We should eliminate all of the self-help and religion books out there and replace them with copies of *Atlas Shrugged.*" I no longer felt a need to examine my mixed emotions about working at the shelter; after all, according to the members of my newly adopted political party, homeless shelters are a part of the problem, just one more weight that keeps men and women pinned to a life of sacrifice, malignant faith, and irrational compromise.

It was Us vs. Them all over again.

I made the jaunt from Westchester County to Gardner, Massachusetts, every few months when blindsided by homesickness. One morning, after having spent the previous night imbibing, I sleepily hit the highway en route to New York.

Somewhere in Connecticut, while listening to the local oldies station, I fell asleep. I awoke to the sound of myself screaming as I drove backwards, scraping along a highway divider, sparks flying everywhere, my hands clenching the wheel in panic.

According to the state trooper who appeared on the scene, I'd drifted into the right lane, bounced off the tire of a sixteen-wheeler, spun around and hit the guardrail like a silver bullet. Aside from a circular black dent on the passenger side and some scratch marks on the driver's door, the car was fine. Surprisingly, so was I. I was ticketed for making a "dangerous lane change," got in the car, and continued my journey back to New York.

I played the events over and over in my head that week and came to the conclusion that there was absolutely no good reason I should be alive. The fact that I'd driven into a sixteen-wheeler and walked away unscathed was nothing short of a miracle; maybe there was a God after all. I pictured Jesus up in Heaven, fiddling with something or other, before turning around and saying "Oh, Lord, what is Karen doing?"

Maybe he stepped in front of the oncoming traffic on Interstate 95 and put his hand out to prevent the other cars from ramming into my out-of-control vehicle. When I related this image to a friend of mine, she gave me the phone number of an Episcopalian priest in White Plains. I made the call, and we set up a time when the two of us would be able to meet and discuss the divine intervention that had spared my life.

I wanted desperately to believe that God had singled me out and stepped in. When I got to her office, however, I began to cry. I ignored the car accident all together, lamenting instead about how much I hated my life in New York. I found myself becoming more and more despondent as the meeting progressed, and I finally excused myself. On the ride back to my rented room, I dismissed the whole "God" idea as silly and returned to the atheistic comfort provided by Ayn Rand.

Perhaps the accident caused me to feel as though I *should* believe in God. Maybe I really wanted to fall on my knees and turn everything over to God, but found the notion too damn frightening. It wasn't as though I were happy, secure, or filled with a sense of purpose; what did I have to lose? My illusory sense of control, that's what.

I never called the priest back.

0 0 0

Upon moving to New York, I'd promised myself that I would stick around for two years. No matter how scared, depressed, lonely or insane I became, I would give the Big Apple two years of my life.

Two years to the day, I threw my meager possessions into my dented Dodge and moved back to Massachusetts.

4

Ridiculous Packaging

Although I tried to place the

blame on society, I wound up back at my parents' house in my early twenties because I hadn't networked, schmoozed, or done anything remotely productive during or immediately following four years of college. Nor was I adapting very well to the "real world." I wanted someone to knock on my door and offer me a high-paying job in which I wouldn't have to work very hard, and I longed for the debauchery and instant, shallow friendships that had marked my years in Amherst.

I was allowed to live at home rent-free for a year while I pursued a career as a freelance cartoonist and graphic artist. Despite my allegiance to Ayn Rand, I did not question or criticize my parents' altruism and self-sacrifice. I did, however, resent the fact that my mother had redecorated my bedroom entirely in pink. My cartoons were finally finding their way into local and national publications such as *Funny Times,* but I was unable to afford my own place; the payment I received too often consisted of "personal satisfaction" or free copies of the magazine.

There's nothing funny about the cartoon business.

I'd been drawing cartoons ever since I could hold a crayon. I'd read *Archie* comics by the bag full, blissfully unaware of the negative female stereotypes being perpetuated by Betty and Veronica. My father brought home copies of *MAD* magazine now and then in my youth, and Patti and I fought over who got the honor of folding the back cover; by high school, I'd graduated to *National Lampoon.*

When I was growing up my favorite *MAD* cartoonist was the late, great Don Martin, whose technique I plagiarized until my own unique style began to evolve. I drew pictures of our teachers to make my classmates laugh and always won the "Bicycle Safety" or "Celebrate Catholic School Week" poster contests sponsored by my school. I walked away from the Senior Assembly at Gardner High with a "Most Artistic" little Oscar award, and doodled compulsively during college lectures. But it would be a few more years until I started attaching punch lines to my drawings.

My first published cartoons were confessional, multi-frame, underground comics that featured yours truly as the main character: cartoon-Karen ponders the inexplicable popularity of pop band The New Kids on the Block; cartoon-Karen tries unsuccessfully to pick someone up in a bar; cartoon-Karen gets drunk by herself in her pink-wallpapered bedroom. And so on. But I found my lead to be too inconsistent; sometimes cartoon-Karen was cocky and confident, and sometimes she was insecure and clueless. So I switched over to the popular single-frame "gag" format. I cheered when Tonya Harding attacked Nancy Kerrigan, and I bowed reverently before O.J. Simpson and Judge Ito. With my sketchbook in hand, the two fallen sports stars showered me with more cartoon fodder than I could contain; the material was practically writing itself. Unfortunately, most of my energy was spent writing cover letters, photocopying cartoons, and stuffing them in manila envelopes.

Think of all of the things you can get away with saying when you tack "I'm just kidding" onto the end of your sentence. Such is the life of a cartoonist. I'll thrust my opinions down your throat, make fun of whomever I wish, hell, I'll even call you an idiot, but it's all in good fun, since "I'm just kidding." The pay is awful, but the freedom is priceless.

My only marketable skills at this point involved making fun of Tonya Harding, chain-smoking cigarettes with homeless junkies, and standing naked in front of art students, so I applied for a modeling position at the local community college in Gardner. The art instructors were thrilled to encounter a woman who not only had studio experience, but who was willing to get naked.

"We have a hard time finding nude models in Gardner," they informed me. "Most of our folks wear a bathing suit or leotard to class, in which case they get $8.00 per hour. We pay $12.00 for the nude sessions."

I wound up modeling for every single figure drawing, painting, and sculpture class at Mount Wachusett Community College that year, much to my parents' chagrin. On the days when I had to wear clothes so that students could practice drawing billowing fabric and shadowy creases, I'd facetiously inquire as to whether or not a quick "flash" would qualify me for the coveted $12.00 rate. I became so comfortable in my work that I engaged students and instructors in discussions about politics and popular culture mid-pose.

"Yep, you're drawing my skinny ass again today," I'd joke as I disrobed for the same old faces. I think that, by the end of the second semester, most of the art students could draw me from memory.

I mostly thought about sex or cartooning while standing around for long stretches of time, my mind racing tirelessly as I tried not to focus on the fact that my foot was falling asleep, or that my left shoulder blade was itchy. When posing for an eight-week sculpture class, however, my imagination went a bit overboard. I stood upon a large lazy-Susan that the instructor rotated every twenty minutes or so while the students transformed their respective lumps of brown clay into diminutive Karen replicas. In order to alleviate the boredom, I created an elaborate fantasy in which I became the "puppet master" of this glorious army of little Karens, an army that could wreak havoc individually or by morphing into one super-human, life-size creature. It would've made a great graphic novel.

It was time to get out of Gardner.

Feeling less adventurous this time around, I returned to Amherst, where I donned the identity of an unapologetic slacker. I moved into a hippie pad that should have been condemned years ago and began a $6.00-per-hour job commandeering the local Kinko's delivery van.

My co-workers were other talented, overeducated, twenty-something drunks who dabbled in novel writing, rock 'n' roll, and/or art by night. We resented the fact that we were forced to perform menial labor in order to pay the rent. We whined about our self-induced poverty while receiving "I love you" checks from our parents to beef up bank accounts diminished by bar-hopping excursions and manic CD-buying binges. We informed customers that Kinko's was only a "time-killing day job" that would do until the book was published or the band got signed. We did not attend church.

I continued to read Libertarian literature and stuck "Vote Libertarian" and "I'd Rather Be Reading Ayn Rand" bumper stickers onto my ailing Dodge K car. In a town that had become so radicalized that nothing was deemed shocking anymore, I relished my role as a shameless agitator. One day, I walked out of Kinko's to find this note under my wiper blade: "If you're so hung up on Ayn Rand, why don't you take that UMass sticker off your car; aren't you opposed to tax-funded institutions?"

He or she had a point. But, like all fanatics, and despite the fact that I hoped to make a living being funny, I lacked a sense of humor regarding the object of my fanaticism. I was angered that the author had had the unmitigated gall to call me out on the fact that my own lifestyle did not always mesh with the philosophies I espoused from the barstool or the bumper.

@ @ @

If asked to name our favorite vice, most of the Kinko's crowd would have said "drinking." However, my co-workers Alice and Ken favored gambling over the pedestrian task of chugging keg beer and passing out on the front lawn. They made frequent excursions to Foxwoods Casino, a garish,

Disney-chic den of iniquity that catered to humankind's basest "get rich quick" desires.

Out of morbid curiosity, I accompanied them one Sunday. I was greeted by tired waitresses in skimpy Indian costumes, their voices ravaged by cigarettes. On that particular day, the lobby was crammed with disabled customers and elderly men and women fresh off the activity bus. When I asked Ken about the rumpled looking, sleepy-eyed casino patrons wandering in and out of the front doors, he informed me that people often slept in their cars between gambling binges. It was all too glamorous.

As I entered the smoky gaming area, I found myself gripped by an odd and disarming sensation. While I'd never experienced my soul as anything more than a metaphor, I became keenly aware of its absence in that casino. It felt as though the negative energy around me were sucking my soul right out of my body. If you've ever gone into an echo-less chamber, then you know what I'm talking about. You shout out a word, only to hear it fall flat and hit the floor. There is no resonance, no depth. We recognize the echo phenomenon only when it is removed. And so it was with my previously unacknowledged soul.

When I got back to Amherst, I tried not to think about my soul anymore.

0 0 0

There was a dearth of joy in my life. My cartoons got bitter and inconsistent, and my drinking escalated. But, from out of the blue, I found temporary salvation in the form of twin fiddles and steel guitars.

Because I fancied myself an edgy *artiste,* I was, for many years, reluctant to explore my affinity for country music. But when I witnessed a TV performance by Dwight Yoakam during my freshman year of college, I no longer had a choice in the matter. I fell in love with the twangy guitars and honky-tonk beat, bought Dwight's *Hillbilly Deluxe* cassette and squirreled it away in a desk drawer; I could not let something as un-hip as a country record sully my carefully-crafted collection of Smiths, Violent Femmes, Beatles, and Velvet Underground albums.

But I couldn't get Dwight out of my mind.

When I surreptitiously purchased another cassette by the singer some years later, I became infatuated with the female vocalist with whom he harmonized on a particular track. Never before had I heard a performer convey such longing and heartache in a song; I believed every word she sang. When Patty Loveless's angelic voice poured forth from my tinny boombox, it was all over, and I was no longer ashamed; I became a loud, proud country music fan.

I dusted off my guitar and mustered up the courage to finally open my mouth. Yes, during drunken college parties, I had shout-sung classic rock tunes like "White Rabbit" for kicks, but I'd never fancied myself a singer. Nor had I fallen into any genre of music that I craved to replicate until I encountered those gutsy, smart, beautiful women with their acoustic guitars, their songs witty and tragic, their vocals passionate. I spent night after night stumbling through tunes about unrequited love, hard drinking, heartache, and joy, trying my damnedest to emulate the catch-in-the-throat, tear-in-your-beer style of my favorite vocalists.

It would be a few more years before Shania Twain and Faith Hill ruined all the fun. Let's face it, Mary Chapin Carpenter and Wynonna would never have gotten contracts if they were just starting out today, as neither can pull off that whole look-sexy-while-rolling-around-in-the-sand-wearing-a-halter-top bit. But for a brief period in the mid-1990s, contemporary country music was truly divine.

I attacked the guitar with an enthusiasm I hadn't known since the days of Doug, my old guitar teacher, and I discovered that my voice wasn't all that bad. It was soft, and not especially powerful, but it was pleasant and more than capable of covering hits by Lorrie Morgan, Suzy Bogguss, and my beloved Patty.

Despite my unfailing atheism, I found myself singing along to songs like *I Know It Was Jesus* by the Nashville Bluegrass Band, and John Berry's dazzling rendition of *Blessed Assurance.* I was especially drawn to "drinkin' and redemption" songs such as Collin Raye's *Little Rock,* Billy Joe Shaver's *If I Give My Soul* and, later, the powerful *Wine Back Into Water* by T. Graham Brown.

Why was I bellowing out lyrics that celebrated the healing power of Jesus' love when I still claimed to be an atheist? Because, as I quickly learned, "God" is as integral to country music as drinkin' and cheatin'. The genre originated in the Bible Belt, after all. Much in the same way that conflicted rap music fans willingly overlook the genre's blatant misogyny because they like the beat, I tolerated the God stuff because I too "liked the beat." Or maybe there *was* something in the lyrics.

God doesn't always utilize burning bushes and thunder claps to get the attention of his wandering flock. Sometimes he speaks in whispers that can be easily drowned out by the click of a remote control or the buzz of a cell phone. And sometimes, as folksinger Dar Williams informs us, "Life gives us lessons sent in ridiculous packaging." God was speaking to me from the twin fiddles, rhinestone jackets, and Fender guitars.

After countless nights of rehearsing, I was ready to unveil the country songs I'd written. My Kinko's co-workers encouraged me to try the open mike night at the Seven Oasis, a smoky, wood-paneled bar where good ol' boys and girls came to hear local bands play Garth Brooks and Lynyrd Skynyrd covers. My pulse pounded in my ears as I broke into my three-song set of originals, which was warmly received. One of the numbers I played was "Rented Room," a melancholy piece that successfully summed up my state of mind at the time:

> I've tried God, and T.V., I ain't got no ninety
> bucks a week for psychotherapy
> I've tried beer and A.A., and the novelty of
> both wore off,
> we went our separate ways
> I've had sex of every style, I've joined self-
> improvement seminars
> and jogged for twenty miles
> I've been up, I've been down, I moved to
> another state
> and in that state another town and

I thought I'd forget about you, I thought I
     could get on with my life
Improve myself and waste some time, fool
     around, expand my mind
And sit in my room and blame myself for
     losing you

There was no "you," per se. Rather, "you" was a composite sketch of all of those things and people from my past who I felt had let me down.

I've had dates, both dumb and blind, and I've
     answered all the personals,
delivered all the lines
It's been hard, and I've been had, I've been
     up the creek, around the bend,
been good and I've been bad, and
I thought I would find another you, to save
     me from the stupid things I do
I thought that I'd be rich by now, a new guitar,
     a fancy house
And not another lonely rented room, where
     I sit and blame myself for losing you

I was still searching for salvation.

I immediately bonded with the other musicians over our shared love for Patsy, Dolly, Johnny, and Willie. The tap beer was cheap, and the bar was frat-boy free. The Seven Oasis became the place to which I felt myself inevitably drawn every weekend.

Once again I'd found a makeshift congregation. We worshiped at the altar of country music and shared in a communal feast of pretzels and beer, the neon Miller signs serving as a poor man's stained-glass window. I dated from within the congregation, my criteria for potential mates involving nothing more than "They've got to be a musician, and they've got to be okay with the fact that I like to drink every night." Needless to say, romantic interests were easy to find.

On the wings of one or two pretty decent original tunes, I found myself lapsing into carefully choreographed and frighteningly detailed fantasies involving my rapid ascent into pop music royalty; the thought of being "ordinary" bothered me to no end. While driving the Kinko's van down Route 9, or in the midst of a particularly boring conversation, I slipped into my make-believe ride on the red carpet, conjuring up images of album covers and witty liner notes. I rehearsed a mock-Grammy Award acceptance speech in my mind, tweaking and rewriting it to ensure that no one was left out. It went something like this:

> *I'd like to thank my parents for buying me my first guitar and for always supporting my crazy dreams. Thank you, Doug, for the guitar lessons. Thank you, Dwight Yoakam, for the inspiration. Thanks to the gang at the Seven Oasis for giving me a chance to sing my songs on stage. Thank you, Lorrie Morgan/ Carlene Carter/Pam Tillis/fill-in-the-blank, for taking a chance on an unknown songwriter. And to all of you struggling songwriters out there, if I can do it, so can you. Thanks!*

I promised myself that I wouldn't forget my humble beginnings or abandon my friends upon winning a Grammy. While receiving said award, I'd be wearing snakeskin boots and a campy rhinestone jacket with matching slacks. In the midst of my newfound fame, I would develop, and then conquer, a terrible heroin addiction, all the while bedding any number of celebrities and fellow tortured artists. Eventually I would settle down and create a musical masterpiece equivalent to Carole King's *Tapestry* or Stevie Wonder's *Songs in the Key of Life.* Cartooning was okay, but it just couldn't compete with my self-destructive rock star fantasy world. Besides, how many cartoonists do you know of that have groupies?

Of course, I never shared these elaborate and embarrassing daydreams with my musical peers. Instead, I mocked those local musicians who recorded CDs in their basements or tried their luck in Nashville or Austin. "Who are they kidding?" I'd sneer while thinking about how hot I looked in tight, leather pants . . . you know, the ones I wore on the cover of my "Greatest Hits" album featuring that duet with Patty Loveless.

4

0 0 0

Rare was the day when I did not drive the Kinko's van while hungover. Upon returning to my hippie pad after work, I'd crack open a beer and spend the first part of the evening creating cartoons. When drunkenness began to affect my ability to draw straight lines, I would switch to the guitar. When the pick fell in the hole, I called it a night.

While I savored the immediate feedback I received from performing, the accolades generated from cartooning were not so tangible. I could gauge the success or lack thereof based on the cartoon's marketability and the money I received, but the actual number of chuckles generated by a particular piece of work would always remain unknown. Incidentally, my favorite rejection letter from this period simply stated, "We laughed, but not hard enough. Try again."

I found myself constantly disappointed that those around me were not dazzled by my status as a professional cartoonist. Because I was terribly shy, I'd hoped that people would be drawn to me due to my minor success in an unusual pursuit. I desperately wanted to shake the "ordinary" label and wanted more than anything to be heard. But the hours I spent each week hunched over my drafting table did not produce lucre or accolades, and I was no longer having fun. I slipped further and further into my fantasy world, where I continued to snort drugs off of hookers' abdomens and pout seductively for photo shoots.

I frequently sulked in the big, cushy chairs at the public library, my favorite destination during those times when I was feeling frustrated and aimless. Besides, my appetite for books was voracious. Mom had given me a library card as soon as I could say "See Spot run," and I am forever grateful for the love of reading she instilled in me. When Gardner's fusty, brick library was closed to make way for a brighter and more efficient facility, Patti and I were crushed. We loved the dark basement that housed the ancient Nancy Drew books and battered Beatrix Potter tomes. We found comfort in the silence and somber mood of the old library; after all, reading was serious business, and the library was no place for clowns, carnivals or festive "Reading Is Fun" posters.

One day, while flipping through periodicals with the phlegmy, retired men at my hometown library, I decided that it was high time to pick a grown-up career. Sure, the cartooning might eventually pay off, but the thought of driving the van at age forty-five while still informing customers that the delivery gig was "just my day job" proved too pathetic to even contemplate. And despite my elaborate rock star daydreams, it was time for a reality check. I hadn't paid my proverbial dues, and, unless I married Bruce Springsteen in the near future, I wasn't going to get a record deal.

"What am I going to do with my life?" I lamented, until the light bulb clicked over my head.

"The library. Of course, I can be a librarian. Damn it, I'm going to library school!"

And I did.

I did not have any relatives in North Carolina; nor did I know anything about the state other than the fact that, in addition to Randy Travis, it produced a whole lot of tobacco. Yet, I felt strangely compelled to move there. I'd grown weary of New England's abandoned factories and bitter winters, and I longed for a radical change of scenery. Having read that North Carolina was a pretty cool place to live, I applied to the state university's campus in Greensboro. The fact that Jodi Messina's single "Heads Carolina, Tails California" had just come out only cemented my decision, though I had flirted with the idea of attending the University of Tennessee in Knoxville because of its proximity to Dollywood. Clearly, then, there was nothing frivolous about my criteria for the perfect graduate school.

As I prepared for my new life in the Old North State, I did not leave the drinking behind. I'd managed to convince myself that I was no longer drinking for the "wrong reasons," and that drunks don't get accepted into graduate school programs. Despite my denial, I continued to abide by a set of strict rules that I'd created years ago regarding my hobby: never begin drinking before 5:00 PM, unless you have been invited to a Labor Day or Fourth of July barbecue;

avoid liquor, and stick to beer as much as possible; only drive when *sort of* drunk, and never drive when *really* drunk; and always tip the bartender. As silly as these rules may appear, they were meaningful to me. With the exception of the bartender rule, they may just have prevented an untimely death.

I left the slacker attitude and tortured artist angst at the Massachusetts-Connecticut state line, as well as my obsession with Ayn Rand. Perhaps my strange passion for Libertarian politics was primarily reactionary, something to separate myself from the hippies and wannabe-communists that thrived in Amherst and Northampton. Maybe I'd finally made peace with my short-lived social work career, and no longer needed *The Fountainhead* to justify my exit. Or maybe I'd just grown tired of worshiping a woman whose view of the world was so one-dimensional, cold, and unrealistic. Regardless, I felt optimistic that a Southern sabbatical might just mellow me out.

Despite snobbish comments such as "Do they have running water in North Carolina?" or "Don't forget to pack your white sheets" from my New England acquaintances, I did not experience much culture shock in my newly adopted state. In fact, I often felt as though I had landed in a cleaner, warmer, and more diverse Worcester, Massachusetts, that happened to sport Waffle House restaurants. I was, however, nearly run out of town on a rail when I asked the shocking question "Who's Richard Petty?"

Since I'd taken out twenty-thousand dollars in student loans for my little library school experiment, I decided to do it right. I schmoozed and networked with professional librarians. I studied hard and banged out "grade A" term papers on my Canon Starwriter word processor. I chatted with my professors every chance I got. At times, when I stopped long enough to catch my breath between part-time library jobs and practicum placements, I barely recognized myself in the seemingly confident career girl I'd become.

Many of the students and staff were from "somewhere else." I befriended Chris, a hard-core atheist from Oregon, and we became inseparable. He was one of those mysterious individuals who'd tried alcohol once but didn't like it.

Regardless, he tolerated my affinity for booze. We grabbed a slot on UNCG's 18-watt radio station, and we created the very silly *Venus & Stork* show. We played the Simpsons' *Songs from the Key of Springfield* CD far too much, and got lots of mileage out of Mel Torme's rendition of "Sunshine Superman." We gave away tins of chewing tobacco during our trivia contests, urging children under the age of eighteen to call in. On some nights, if wrapped entirely in aluminum foil while standing on a roof within a half-mile radius of the station, you could actually hear us.

It was during my first year of graduate school that I hoisted my last beer. First and foremost, I possessed enough insight to grasp that, if I remained in a numb, drunken state, I would never muster up enough courage to walk away from the latest dysfunctional relationship into which I had willingly entered. Secondly, I had finally found a career opportunity that looked promising. I felt optimistic about my future, and didn't want alcohol to hurt my prospects. Finally, I was smart enough to realize that my luck was bound to run out at some point.

I'd driven drunk on many occasions. As a result of booze, I'd sprained my knee twice, chipped a tooth, narrowly escaped a drug bust, committed acts of vandalism, and acted like an ass in more instances than I care to discuss. I drove home on many a night with one eye closed in an attempt to ward off double vision. How long would it be before I got a D.U.I. or, even worse, killed a fellow driver? How long before I really hurt myself or wound up in a dangerous situation that I could not control? How long before I cut off my emotions altogether?

I believe that my decision to quit drinking was the first major step on the road back to God. In the same way that one cannot have a meaningful and satisfying conversation with a person who has just consumed a six-pack, I do not think it's beneficial to talk to God when one of the parties is slurring. Meaningful conversations lead to meaningful relationships. How can we listen for the still, small voice when our minds have been dulled with Budweiser? How can we

get to know ourselves and God through prayer and meditation when we keep nodding off?

After only a week of sobriety, I ended my toxic romantic
relationship. I stopped hanging out with people who use
"party" as a verb and began taking more of an interest in my
health, eating habits, and personal appearance. Through
sheer stubbornness, I remained sober throughout the initial
sleepless nights and detox symptoms. I still fantasized about
getting drunk. In restaurants, I watched enviously as men
and women laughed over cocktails. I could smell booze from
across a crowded room and felt appalled when diners care-
lessly left a half-finished bottle of beer behind as they
departed for the night. While the desire to drink has certainly diminished over the years, it has never entirely left me.

As I struggled to figure out how to live life without the aid
of alcohol, the formerly beer-filled, God-shaped hole in my
soul remained bone dry.

5

"Life Is Suffering"

Franco-Americans aren't the only
demographic group that could benefit from the services of
a reputable public relations firm. Librarians have been the
brunt of lame jokes and unfair stereotypes ever since they
first started flirting with the Dewey Decimal System.
You've seen the librarian archetype—she's a curmudgeonly,
asexual, bespectacled crone with cat's-eye glasses, a furrowed brow, and a tight bun who says "Shhhhhhh" a great
deal. In fact, she looks like Dana Carvey's infamous Church
Lady character.

Advertising agents, screenwriters, and comedians (cartoonists, too) who constantly revive this tired cliché obvi-
ously haven't set foot in a public library for some years.
Libraries are anything but quiet these days, and the new
crop of professionals is more concerned with keeping
abreast of cutting-edge information technology than in
shushing noisy patrons. Sure, the profession does attract
some mousy, bookish loners, but the same could be said
about file clerks, elementary school teachers, data entry spe-
cialists, sociology professors, social workers, and just about
every other occupation that does not include "sports,"
"entertainment," or "model" in its title.

Yes, we librarians get a little defensive sometimes. If you
really want to anger a professional librarian, go up to one
and say, "Why do you need a master's degree to shelve

books?" But be warned—you know those cat's-eye glasses we all wear? They transform into deadly Ninja disks.

Upon receipt of my master's degree in library studies, I landed an entry-level management job at a small public library in Alamance County, North Carolina. In a tone most condescending, I informed friends and family that I'd died and wound up in Mayberry, U.S.A. The gals with whom I worked had all been born in the county. They married guys from the county and would probably be buried in the county. I kept a safe emotional distance from my employees because I thought I could not possibly have anything in common with these small-town soccer moms. Of course, I was wrong.

Having spent my entire adulthood associating with lapsed Catholics and atheists, I was caught off guard to find myself surrounded by Christians who did not require prefixes like "former," "lapsed," or "recovering." As in most small North Carolina towns, virtually everyone who lived there belonged to a church. So I smiled politely when patrons talked about their congregation or recommended the latest Christian fiction title to me. And I did not invoke that whole "separation of church and state" issue when the staff decorated a Christmas tree in December, as no one in the community made a fuss. Apparently, Alamance County is not an ACLU stronghold.

On my first day of work, an elderly gentleman in overalls placed a glass jar containing a dead snake on the circulation desk and said, "This snake fell on my head this morning; can you tell me what it is?" If I work as a librarian for thirty more years, I doubt that I'll ever get a reference question quite as colorful as that first one.

But I digress . . .

I became intrigued by one of my employees, a sweet and somewhat shy part-timer named Brenda, who never spoke ill of others or rolled her eyes when dealing with difficult patrons. Despite having suffered tremendous losses in her life, I can't recall ever having heard her complain. I remember thinking to myself "I want that; I want what Brenda has." I discovered that she was a Christian only because she once asked us if we'd like to purchase Brunswick stew as part of her church's fundraiser. She never uttered the words "Jesus" or "saved." She didn't need to.

And then a funny thing happened. I began to meet other cool Christians. There was that warm, funny guy who worked part-time as a magician; I learned later, from a co-worker, that he was a minister. There were the sweet, smart, Christian ladies in the book discussion group I facilitated who practiced random acts of kindness and befriended the lonely widow in our midst. My supervisor, a devout Methodist, proudly proclaimed that she was pro-choice, pro-Clinton, and pro-Jimmy Buffet.

My feelings about Christianity were still too muddled for me to sit down with the book group ladies, my co-workers, or my supervisor to inquire about their faith or pick their brains regarding God. Instead, I bonded with Paula, a library patron and former Catholic from Illinois who had become enamored by New Age religion. She spoke of karma, meditation, and other sexy sounding phenomena about which I wasn't familiar. She practiced some sort of "healing touch therapy" in which she channeled positive energy into her clients, both human and equine, curing them of aches and pains. I played devil's advocate with her on our lunch dates, attributing near-death experiences to neuron impulses and claiming that visions were nothing more than wishful thinking. But my curiosity regarding alternative religion had been piqued.

And then I found the book that would change my life.

It was a Friday afternoon; surprisingly, I had nothing on hand to read over the weekend. So I wandered over to the "New Books" shelf and reached for the one with the most interesting cover, which happened to be *Traveling Mercies* by Anne Lamott. The book had received positive reviews from both *Library Journal* and the *New York Times,* so I checked it out and dropped it into my bag.

Yes, the author was a Christian, but she was unlike any Christian I'd ever knowingly met. Anne swore like a sailor and did not always succeed in loving her neighbors as herself. She'd spent most of her adult life drinking heavily and experimenting with drugs, and, before she accepted Jesus into her life, thought that Christianity was a bunch of crap. She explains her conversion experience as follows:

> After a while, as I lay there, I became aware
> of someone with me, hunkered down in the
> corner. . . The feeling was so strong that I actually
> turned the light on for a moment to make sure
> no one was there—of course, there wasn't. But
> after a while, in the dark again, I knew beyond
> any doubt that it was Jesus. I felt him as surely
> as I feel my dog lying nearby as I write this.

The next paragraph sounds like something I might have written in my sobriety journal in college:

> And I was appalled. I thought about my life
> and my brilliant hilarious progressive friends,
> I thought about what everyone would think of
> me if I became a Christian, and it seemed an
> utterly impossible thing that simply could not
> be allowed to happen. I turned to the wall and
> said out loud, "I would rather die."

But she finally gave in.

> . . .I stood there a minute, and then I hung
> my head and said, "Fuck it: I quit." I took a long
> deep breath and said out loud, "All right. You
> can come in."

This was hardly St. Paul's conversion on the road to Damascus, but to me it was pure poetry. After reading Anne's words, I was finally ready to admit that maybe, just maybe, there might be something to this spirituality thing. For the first time in many years, I allowed myself to entertain the notion that perhaps everything can't be explained with neat little equations or longwinded essays in academic journals.

Unfortunately, my attitude toward Christianity was still "I would rather die."

When one stumbles across a profoundly influential book, song, or person, it is tempting to believe that God himself rearranged the cosmos that day to ensure that the fateful encounter would take place. Personally, I believe that God inspires authors, songwriters, and artists to create works like *Traveling Mercies* every day so that angry atheists and well-meaning but confused seekers may "accidentally" discover them. I believe that God uses everything from the serious to the frivolous to connect with us; some folks have caught a glimpse of the Divine while listening to the words of a learned theologian; others have done so while scratching a dog's belly or watching an ABC *Movie of the Week*.

God has strewn tools, agents, and roadmaps all over the earth, but, most of the time, we look right through them. Or maybe we're holding one in the palms of our hands but haven't got a clue as to the item's value. Had I encountered *Traveling Mercies* in my teens or early twenties I would have seen it as nothing more than a flat surface upon which to roll a joint. Had I met Brenda in the dorms, I'd have viewed her simply as a "goodie two-shoes," a sweet but boring gal to be smiled at but ultimately dismissed. How many of "God's agents" did I breeze past in my youth? How many potentially helpful tools did I toss aside, too selfish and preoccupied to see through the sometimes ridiculous packaging?

A few weeks later, confused about what to do with this new open-mindedness regarding spirituality, I browsed through the library's sparse selection of non-Christian spirituality titles. My eyes drifted immediately toward the book with the most exotic-sounding title: *The Tibetan Book of Living and Dying*. It was an odd shape. It was orange. I grabbed it.

I was immediately taken with Tibetan Buddhism, the most colorful of the religion's various sects. The author, Sogyal Rinpoche, spoke of exotic phenomena like mantras, rebirth, and the "continuity of mind," the latter referring to the belief that consciousness does not die with the physical body but survives into the next life. He proclaimed that we are the sum total of all of our previous actions from all of our previous lifetimes, and he urged his readers to question the stagnant ways of thinking to which we'd become accustomed so that we might advance to a higher level of consciousness.

With each page I read, a new vocabulary unfolded before me, a vocabulary that didn't include the word *sin* or a lot of stuffy *thou shalt nots.* But it was the most basic tenet of the Buddha's teachings that struck the loudest chord in my brain: "Life is suffering." It was so pure, so simple, so harsh; Siddhartha Gautama didn't pull any punches. Life is suffering.

He didn't leave his disciples hanging, however. The Buddha explained that the greatest cause of earthly suffering is desire. We desire people. We desire objects. We desire status, fame, wealth. Yet, because everything is impermanent, desire will only lead to disappointment and frustration. I was blown away by this "radical" view, despite the fact that Jesus had covered much of the same ground in his own teachings.

I sought out books on meditation, the most effective means of cleaning out the clutter and white noise that cloud our minds and prevent us from getting in touch with our perfect, inner "Buddha nature." I gladly accepted the philosophy that there is no external God per se; because perfect wisdom already exists within us, the Buddha taught, we can all become our own saviors. And if we become our own saviors, then God becomes redundant.

I had discovered an atheistic religion. I was in Heaven.

——————— ⟁ ———————

Despite the Buddha's teachings on the absurdity of lusting after material objects, I found myself buying as much Buddhist stuff as possible. It started out with a silver Buddha amulet that I proudly wore around my neck. Then there were posters, Buddha statues, and books. I found some prayer flags for a good price, and I grabbed a batch of Tibetan deity postcards at a New Age shop in Carrboro. If I'd found a "Buddhism Rocks!" t-shirt, I would've bought that too. Much in the same way that I'd once proclaimed my love for the Beatles, David Bowie, Karl Marx, and Ayn Rand on everything from bumper stickers to cigarette lighters, I wanted to wear my new faith on my sleeve. I even considered getting a Tibetan mantra tattooed on my forearm, until I remembered that I preferred scars to tattoos.

I bought a mat and continued to research the finer points of meditation. The experts all agreed that the goal of one's practice should not be zoned-out bliss, because meditation is not a passive act. They also seemed to agree that one should not suppress his or her thoughts during mediation. Rather, we should acknowledge these thoughts, embrace them, and then let them go. As a writer, my first reaction was, "But what if a really great idea pops into my head; shouldn't I run with it?" Of course, the things that usually popped into my head were no deeper than grocery lists or rock star fantasies, but I liked to believe that my brain was a font of profundity that should not be ignored.

It was time to get my head out of the books and my butt on the mat. As a person who possesses an unhealthy amount of nervous energy, however, I never quite got the hang of meditation. Right at the moment in which I thought I'd cleared the clutter from my mind, the Oscar Meyer Weiner jingle or that catchy theme song from *Welcome Back, Kotter* would appear. I'd acknowledge it, embrace it, let it go, and watch it tumble right back into my brain. "Welcome back, your dreams were your ticket out. . . ."

The silence was thick and brutal. My feet fell asleep, my nose itched, and my bony behind ached; it was a lot like art modeling, minus the money and nudity. I tried visualization and chanting "Om Mani Padme Hum," the divine mantra of love and compassion, but enlightenment remained elusive.

The Buddha had a tremendous amount of respect for the religious beliefs of others. Unlike many insecure holy men, he never claimed to have all the answers. So I sought out books about Hinduism's colorful pantheon of gods and goddesses. I explored the writings of Paramahansa Yogananda, author of *Autobiography of a Yogi*. I read the poems of Rumi

and peeked at the pamphlets at the local Hare Krishna vegetarian restaurant. And as long as I could approach it from a
purely academic stance, I even explored Christianity a bit.

Buddhists view Jesus as "a buddha," which simply means
"an enlightened one," much in the same way that they view
Krishna and Muhammad. In fact, some authors argue that,
during Jesus' "missing years," he was hanging out in India,
copping all of the Buddha's good material. Thus, I gained a
new respect for Jesus, but I was not yet ready to embrace
him as the Son of God. He was just another ingredient in
the religion soup I began stirring up.

@ @ @

A real, live Tibetan lama, decked out in requisite saffron
robes and sandals, made an appearance one Saturday at a
small Episcopalian church in Greensboro. Having placed
our shoes at the door, we sat on pillows and stared in rapt
attention as he fingered a string of prayer beads and
proclaimed the Dharma. Afterwards, when a disciple
announced the formation of a Tibetan Buddhist prayer
group, my name was first on the list.

The group was composed primarily of white, middle-class
baby boomers. We meditated and chanted in Tibetan, which
meant I had absolutely no idea what I was praying about;
I suppose this is how Catholics felt back in the days of
the Latin Mass. The folks who attended weren't all that
friendly, and, much like those A.A. meetings years before, I'd
leave feeling lost and depressed. Should I meditate more?
Should I purchase a bigger amulet? Should I shave my
head? I became convinced that I was doing something
wrong and drifted away from the group altogether.

Eventually, Buddhism evolved into more of an intellectual pursuit than a spiritual one. I still told people that I was
a Buddhist, and that I abstained from eating meat for religious reasons, but my heart was no longer in the teachings.
I drifted deeper into my religion soup, wondering when
someone or something would nudge me out of my spiritual
stupor.

Regardless, I am forever grateful for the wisdom that I attained during my brief dance with Buddhism. The Buddha and his disciples taught me to slow down and look for "the divine" in the details. His teachings encouraged me to pray for those people I disliked and to treat everyone as potential buddhas, no matter how dysfunctional their lives might appear to be. And, because of the religion's insistence that all creatures should be treated with respect and kindness, I remain a devout vegetarian. The prayer flags and posters may be packed away in a cardboard box, but my refusal to eat anything with legs has never waned.

I've yet to give up leather. But since I only wear shoes and jackets made from cows who've committed suicide, I shouldn't feel guilty, right?

6
Spiritual Narcissism

The medium was an affable fellow. He was thin and slightly effeminate, his manner laid back, his speech slow and deliberate. His followers were mostly upper-middle-class white women in their forties and fifties, and he knew them all by name. My friend Maggie, a lapsed Catholic who enjoyed dabbling in the New Age arts, invited me to sit in on a session; the sociologist in me couldn't refuse. Despite my new open-mindedness regarding those mysterious, spiritual forces that swirl around us at every waking moment, I was still suspicious about psychics and mediums. In fact, I subjected Maggie to a very bad but relevant joke on the way over to mask my discomfort.

"Maggie, what do you call a dwarf fortune teller who escapes from prison?"

"I don't know, Karen, what *do* you call a dwarf fortune teller who escapes from prison?"

"A small medium at large."

Ba-dum-bump.

When everyone was seated, the hostess asked us to write one "personal" and one "universal" question on the small pieces of paper she handed us. After much dithering about what constituted a "universal" question, we got to work and placed our papers in two separate bowls. Upon selecting a question (the writer's identity remained anonymous throughout), the medium closed his eyes, rubbed the paper between his fingertips and channeled the spirit with whom he communicated. He was a great showman.

The "personal" questions mainly involved lost pets or the search for Mr. Right. Sometimes the spirit's message was blunt. "No, the love of your life is *not* waiting for you around the corner," the medium might proclaim, or, "Sorry, Muffy the cat won't be coming home." But the proverbial glass was always half full. If the man of her dreams was not due to appear anytime soon, it was only because the seeker needed to first discover that she was a warrior princess, a strong woman who did not need a man to complete her. If Muffy the cat had been run over by an SUV, the owner was assured that the gray tabby was now living in a "much better place." And so on.

My personal question was "Do my stomach aches have anything to do with the abdominal surgeries I had as a child, and will I need to undergo surgery?" In the past few months, I'd had three bouts of severe abdominal pain, vomiting, and diarrhea. I was also looking pretty gaunt, sort of like a female Keith Richards. Because of my long history of illness, I worried that the symptoms might be harbingers of terrible things to come, even though my doctor and everyone around me insisted that I just had the flu.

"My spirit guide is saying something about a course in positive thinking," he announced, his eyes closed tight. "And I'm hearing something about a conflict between you and your mother. Yes, that's the source." He then moved on to another question about a pet.

I am a firm believer in the power of positive thinking. We've all been around profoundly negative people, and their energy is stifling; you can practically cut it with a butter knife. But there's also something to be said for good old Western medicine, as it saved my life on a number of occasions. And as far as the "conflict with your mother" statement goes, if everyone who had issues with their mom developed flu-like symptoms, we'd all be wearing galoshes.

But just when I was about to dismiss this whole psychic thing as a sham, the guy redeemed himself. He went around the room and asked his spirit guide to assign "archetypes" for each of us. When my turn arose, he looked me straight in the eye and said "Your archetype is the Fool." Before I had a chance to say, "Hey, I resent that," he expounded:

"You're on stage, making people laugh and juggling lots

of balls at once, but you're very concerned about where they'll land. And you're very concerned about what the audience thinks."

"Wow," I thought to myself, "I *am* an insecure person who draws funny cartoons and plays the guitar so that people will like me. And, despite being an artist, I'm incredibly uptight. He's figured me out! Maybe he really *can* communicate with this spirit guide of his."

It was an "oh wow" moment, the kind of thing that keeps desperate seekers coming back for more.

As Maggie and I drove home, I began to view the whole spectacle as rather pointless. Had we really gained anything by having been assigned an archetype? Had we grown spiritually by being told those things we already knew? Was the world a better place now because we learned that our beloved former pet had attained nirvana, or that, despite our unassuming demeanor, we're all really Xenas and Vampire Slayers waiting to come out and play? And who was this mysterious spirit who had answered our deep, dark questions anyway? Was he malevolent? Did he have an agenda? Should we trust him?

In my confusion about all things New Age, I visited a neo-pagan co-worker of mine named Emma. When I asked her to sum up paganism in a nutshell, she mumbled a few things about God being present in the trees and rivers, and spoke of the sacredness of "Mother Earth." She went on to tell me that there is no definitive pagan text akin to the Bible or the Koran, and that the only moral tenet to which she adheres is "Do no harm."

"So what do y'all do when a group of pagans get together? Do you pray? Do you chant? Do you dance around a fire?"

"We make it up as we go along," Emma replied.

I've yet to hear a better description of New Age practice.

@ @ @

I said "farewell" to the small-town charm of Alamance County and accepted a more challenging and lucrative management position in a much larger public library system. As I threw myself deeper into my career, spirituality got pushed to the back of the bus. It would pop up in conversations and worm its way into my brain now and then, motivating me to do things like pay good money to talk to mediums, but my spiritual journey was, for all intents and purposes, dead in the water.

I continued to play the occasional musical gig, but I longed for a duo partner with whom to harmonize and explore more challenging songs; let's face it, tackling Simon and Garfunkel's greatest hits as a solo vocalist gets lonely after a while. I found this potential partner during a library-sponsored sing-a-long on the children's ward at Moses Cone Hospital. Shannon could belt out tunes like Linda Ronstadt, and sing harmony like Don Everly's bastard child. We traded Indigo Girls and Gram Parsons CDs, camped it up with old Barbara Mandrell songs and complimented each others' originals. We formed a duo, and I convinced myself that two-part harmony and audience adulation would finally fill that gaping, God-shaped hole in my soul.

As Shannon and I got to know each other better, she revealed her spiritual beliefs to me. Yet another lapsed-Catholic who'd abandoned Christianity, Shannon placed her faith in tarot cards, astrology, past-life regression therapy, and psychics. We spent many a practice break discussing the superiority of Eastern religious philosophy over its Western counterpart.

But despite the exotic accouterments and sexy sounding beliefs, I just couldn't bring myself to embrace New Age the way my well-meaning friends did. I could not help but notice that, despite bashing organized religion every chance they got, they had no problem plucking out the fluffier, less threatening pieces from the stuffy, sacred texts they scorned. By claiming to be "spiritual" as opposed to "religious," they exempted themselves from the discipline and sacrifice inherent in most organized traditions. "Spirituality" does not demand that its adherents pay attention to the needs of their earthly brothers and sisters as they fumble toward enlightenment; rather, the focus is on the seeker, his or her one-on-one relationship to God, and the individual's own personal quest for happiness.

Perhaps a desire for instant spiritual gratification is what makes many New Age practices so appealing and accessible.

For example, why would anyone want to spend countless hours silently contemplating life's big questions when a psychic or medium can provide answers on the spot? Why face uncomfortable truths about yourself and take responsibility for the poor choices you've made when they can be attributed to bad karma from past lives? Why worry about all that "discipline" and "sacrifice" stuff when you can pick and chose your truths, "making it up as you go along"?

I didn't yet know what I needed, but I had a pretty good idea that it wasn't New Age. Making it up as I go along is what got me into trouble in college, back when I played by my own rules and modified my morals depending on my mood. I had enough insight to recognize that it wouldn't be wise for a self-absorbed artist like myself to embark upon a path that was all about "me."

For all intents and purposes, I had "made it." I held a secure, well-paying job that I didn't hate. I made up one half of a terrific musical duo. I owned a new Honda Civic and had opened up my first Roth IRA. But I was tired of living in thin-walled, noisy apartment complexes managed by unsympathetic landlords. I decided that my quest for happiness would be complete if I became a homeowner. Armed with a number of how-to books from the library, I began the lengthy process of finding the perfect house.

During my search, I was amazed by the complete lack of books I encountered in the houses I visited. Sure, one or two homeowners had purchased those faux leather-bound Classics of Western Civilization volumes to fill up built-in bookcases, but, because of the perfect condition of the spines, I knew they'd never been cracked. Big screen televisions, however, were abundant. One rather portly couple had even suspended a TV from the ceiling of their bedroom, which made me recall my various hospital stints. I suppose that librarians notice these things more than the average home hunter, since our job security hinges on the assumption that people like to read.

But I digress . . .

I convinced myself that buying a house would provide me with the peace of mind I so desired. No longer would I be forced to tolerate buffoons blasting Phish next door at two o'clock in the morning, or suffer as rowdy college kids hosted soirees while I tried to read. No, I wouldn't just be buying a house, I'd be purchasing peace of mind. The vinyl siding would buffer me against the noisy, ignorant, unwashed masses with whom I was forced to cohabitate. Buying a house would allow me to hide *and* build equity; who could ask for more?

I found a cute three-bedroom, two-bath ranch house with a garage and fenced in backyard that was listed in my meager price range, and I took out a thirty-year mortgage for my very own slice of suburban heaven. Instead of providing me with comfort, however, my beloved house became a very expensive albatross. No, the pipes didn't burst, and the roof did not collapse in a dusty heap. I did not encounter a termite infestation or learn that my plot of land had once been a sacred Indian burial ground à la *Poltergeist*. Rather, as I stood in the center of the living room, a reality more terrifying than bad plumbing hit me like a swift kick to the kidneys.

"I've sold out."

I sat down and began to cry. Karen Favreau, the tortured artist, writer, and former slacker had sold her soul for the whitewashed land of SUVs, neighborhood potlucks, and manicured lawns. Carole King had warned me about this, hadn't she? Had I not listened carefully enough to "Pleasant Valley Sunday," her scathing indictment against those suburban rows of houses that are all the same?

As I stared at my new Kenmore refrigerator and washer/dryer combo, I crumbled beneath the weight of my possessions. I was trapped. I thought about the old days, back when I could throw all of my possessions into my Dodge K Car, give a two-week notice at whatever crappy job I was holding and hit the road. I'd slept on hand-me-down futons, made do with milk-crate bookshelves and got by just fine on two hundred dollars a week. Now I owned major appliances. Had I ignored the Buddha's teachings about "desire" while succumbing to the empty promises sold and packaged by Sears?

How could I be edgy in such a sterile environment? How could I write the great American novel amidst the monumental mediocrity into which I'd willingly subjected myself? How could I ponder humanity's existential angst when I found myself getting excited over things like weed-whackers and the Swiffer? Perfectly trimmed lawns and clean floors don't inspire artists. I belonged in New York City with the freaks and the punks and the subway cars that smelled like urine. But here I was in the suburbs, losing my edge, bit-by-bit, piece-by-piece.

In an effort to regain this diminishing edge, I drove across town to the King Pin tattoo parlor and piercing emporium to inquire about getting my navel pierced. A young woman with enough metal in her face to pick up FM radio showed me a tray of lovely navel rings and then asked for a look at my belly button.

"Oh, Honey," she announced in her sweetest Southern drawl, "I can't do anything with that!"

Apparently, my surgical scars had mutated my navel into a shape and depth that was not conducive to piercing.

"If I put one in, it'll fall right out by tomorrow."

I thanked her for her honesty and left the King Pin in a funk. My symbolic attempt at reclaiming my wasted youth had failed; I would remain un-pierced.

And then, in the midst of my mid-life meltdown, the noisy teenagers began to congregate in front of my driveway.

A loudmouthed girl in the neighborhood named Tammy developed a crush on the slacker who rented a house across from me. As a result, the edge of my lawn became her new hangout, a command post to which other teenagers were drawn, until my block began to resemble the line outside of the MTV Video Music Awards. So much for the peace of mind I'd sought.

Normal people feel joy when they buy their first home and furnish it with nice things. Normal people take pleasure in the sound of laughter and the sight of kids frolicking good-naturedly outside their window. I, however, felt tension and despair. In order to better understand my bizarre aversion to teenagers, success, and major appliances, I swallowed my pride and called a shrink.

6

I'd seen a therapist during my beer-drenched freshman year of college, but had been imbibing too much to benefit from our sessions. In fact, therapy had become a bit like confession; I'd binge drink, do something stupid, and then tell my therapist about it. I didn't realize that one must suffer discomfort when trying to improve one's life. As long as I was numb from drinking, therapy didn't do a whole lot of good. I'd refused to allow myself to squirm.

But things were different now. For starters, I was sober. And, unlike my state of mind fifteen years before, I truly wanted to get better. I was willing to accept the pain that accompanies growth, and the fear that's an indelible part of peering into your troubled past.

In the meantime, I closed the blinds and turned up the music.

"This Tammy girl, is she about the same age as you were when you underwent all that surgery?"

Cue to dramatic music; Karen slaps her forehead with the *palm of her hand.*

"Of course! I resent the fact that she's out having fun because I was busy contemplating my own death at her age, just like I resented that girl in the body cast at Mass General who joked with the nurses."

I was matched with a no-nonsense therapist who didn't tolerate self-pity or sulking. If there was a topic about which I didn't wish to expound, she gently pushed until I gave in and spilled the beans. Meagan was exactly the kind of person I needed in my corner, someone who wouldn't fall for my games and elaborate defense mechanisms, someone who could see through my thick black metaphorical biker jacket. Touchy-feely works for some people, but, at this point in my life, I needed tough love.

After the Tammy epiphany, we dissected the troubled relationship I had with my emotions. I recalled a Carlene Carter concert I'd attended eight or nine years before, back in the days when Johnny Cash's stepdaughter was scoring

Ridiculous Packaging

hits as opposed to scoring heroin. My friend Brian and I drank beer and danced all that afternoon, basking in the glow of the July fourth sun and Carlene's quirky country pop. When the show wrapped up, we joined the gaggle of fans milling about her tour bus, all of us hoping to grab an autograph. Much to our surprise, the singer's manager came out, pointed to Brian and me, and said, "Carlene wants to meet you."

We held our breath as we entered the bus, our CDs and sharpies clutched to our chests. The star emerged in sweat pants and a t-shirt, gave us a big hug, and said, "I could see that the two of you were really getting into my show. It's people like you that make it all worthwhile!"

We practically floated back to Gardner as we relived the glorious moment when queen Carlene hugged us and signed our CDs. When I dropped Brian off and got back to my room, however, I sank into a deep depression. It didn't make any sense, but, with Meagan's help, I came to understand that I really didn't know how to handle joy. For the most part, the only intense feelings I'd ever experienced had been bad ones. So when intense *positive* feelings arose, I withdrew, got depressed, and felt numb.

"It's what you know," she said, "It's safe. And it's not like you've had a lot of practice expressing emotions at home."

Some months later, a paragraph in Danny Bonaduce's *Random Acts of Badness* caught my eye. Yes, I said Danny Bonaduce. While I enjoy serious literature and critically acclaimed titles, I also indulge in the occasional tell-all celebrity memoir, my last remaining guilty pleasure since giving up alcohol, cigarettes, and the consumption of animal flesh. Anyway, the former child star of *The Partridge Family* writes the following:

> My theory is, possibly, just possibly, I started taking drugs because I don't know "how to feel"—whether that involves feeling good or bad . . . It was as if I was emotionally immune but still able to function outwardly as an emotional human being . . . On the other hand, give four normal people and me a handful of Quaaludes and we will all feel exactly the same way: "rubbery."

Oddly, while on drugs, I felt exactly the
same way as other people—as long as the other
people were on drugs.

So I wasn't the only person who had such troubles. I felt
validated. Yes, life gives us lessons sent in ridiculous packaging, indeed.

Meagan and I explored my stoic childhood, my melancholy demeanor, and my former affinity for alcohol. I talked
about the spiritual void in my life, and the shame I felt in
abandoning Buddhism after having made such a big deal
about my supposed beliefs. We talked about the emotional
distance between my parents and myself, and the way in
which Patti and I constantly bickered, despite our love for
each other. And I tried to make peace with the terrible physical and emotional pain I endured when I was cut up and
sewn back together as a teenager.

After a few sessions, I found myself making terrific
progress. But those damn teenagers still bothered me.

7

Earth Is Crammed with Heaven

There's no right way to have a

spiritual awakening. For some people, the conversion experience comes about as a gradual opening of the heart, a seemingly unspectacular, subtle change in perception or desire. For others, the awakening is dramatic and fully ethereal. People use words like *light* or *electricity* to give form to that which is indescribable. Metaphors are invoked, adjectives are exhausted, and emotions are unbound. The light they discuss might be warm and inviting, or sudden and intense, the wind a gentle breeze or a violent gust. The awakening could be anticipated or unbidden, welcomed or rejected, viewed as the start of a new life or nothing more than a particularly vivid acid flashback.

By the same token, there's no *wrong* way to have a spiritual awakening, though I'd approach anything involving snake-handling, Madonna, or L. Ron Hubbard with extreme caution.

My friend Dana discovered the whole of God's glory in a leaf while hiking one morning. As she gazed at the intricate web of veins that fanned throughout the everyday object in her hand, she felt as if she were viewing life for the very first time. There was immense gratitude in her heart for this flash of the Divine, and she vowed to explore her relationship with God in a profound and serious manner. Yet Dana's enthusiasm began to wane almost as soon as she drove away from the mountain. When she returned to her busy life with all of its demands and distractions, leaves went back to being mere stems and petioles, nothing but objects to be raked up and gathered in trash bags come autumn. And God retreated back into that inaccessible place from which he'd temporarily and unexpectedly emerged.

Then there's conversion poster-boy Paul, the persecutor formerly known as Saul. As our hero traveled to Damascus, Jesus spoke to him from a flash of light so intense that it caused temporary blindness. Upon recovering his sight, Paul went on to carry Jesus' name to the Gentiles, thus changing history as we know it.

My own awakening occurred on an unusually warm afternoon in late February. Despite the progress I'd been making in therapy, I still felt anxious when I pulled onto my street to find the teenagers milling about. While I understood the source of my angst from a rational perspective, it still lingered like a festering sore that simply wouldn't scab over. I stormed past the small army in front of my house, slammed the front door behind me and threw my briefcase onto the couch, feeling as though I might crumble or explode at any minute. And then, without really thinking about what I was doing, I knelt down beside the couch and asked God to comfort me.

I'll be damned if he didn't do just that.

As the plea escaped my lips, I heard a still, small voice say "Talk to them." But the speaker didn't just say the words. No, for lack of a better explanation, God *breathed* them through me, and I experienced the statement with every one of my senses, every fiber, every muscle and every nerve ending; it burrowed into my bones.

I remember rising from the couch with a dazed expression on my face. I proceeded to pace around the living room, smiling like an idiot, walking in circles and muttering under my breath.

"I'll talk to the teenagers, of course. It makes perfect sense."

In that moment, I was completely free of anxiety. I knew implicitly that, if I heeded the advice of the speaker, then everything would be okay. In fact, I'd never felt so sure about anything in my life. I was absolutely convinced of the speaker's authority, and therefore I was absolutely at peace. I knew. I *just knew.*

I slept like a baby that night.

After work the next day, I spotted Tammy walking alone, sans her entourage.

"Hey, have you got a minute?" I asked.

"Sure." She seemed glad that I was actually acknowledging her existence instead of just glaring wordlessly.

"Um . . . it kind of bugs me when y'all gather on my lawn like that."

"I'm sorry. We won't do it anymore."

"And when you rang my doorbell and ran the other night . . . do you guys dislike me or anything?"

"Oh, no . . . my stupid little sister did that. I'm sorry. I'll talk to her."

"No problem. Look, if you ever just want to chat or something, just stop by, okay?"

"Sure."

We smiled and parted ways. She wasn't a bad kid after all. I regretted not having asked her to name the *Breakfast Club* character with whom she most closely identified.

On the surface, my collision with God seemed very practical and matter-of-fact: I'd had a problem, I'd asked for help, God had offered a suggestion and I'd taken his advice; the future looked promising. I could've said, "Thanks, Big Guy," and then ignored God until the next problem for which I needed help arose.

But I'd been changed. And, more important, I knew that God existed. Not as a generic white light, not as the vague "absolute" of theosophy, but as God in all of his glory, the God of my childhood, the God of the Bible, the God that loved all of his children, even the sinners, even the snotty intellectuals who argued against his existence. Because of the profound sense of peace I'd felt during the encounter, I understood that true joy can only come through commun-ion with God. I'd tasted true peace, and I wanted more.

Yes, all of this knowledge flooded into me in a span of one-and-a-half seconds, the total amount of time it took God to say, "Talk to them." And, no, it makes absolutely no sense from a rational point of view.

———————   ◢   ———————

We live in a world that loves the *kaboom!* We embrace the dramatic, the bold, the over-the-top; we revel in the moment. Nowhere is this more evident than in Hollywood love stories. Take *The Wedding Singer* (*please,* take *The Wedding Singer*). Adam Sandler is in love with Drew Barrymore, who is betrothed to a cocky, cruel and unfaith-ful bore. After much levity and a couple of Van Halen jokes, Drew finally sees the light. She dumps the idiot boyfriend and leaps into Adam's arms as the audience cheers. I think the movie ends with the two of them kissing on an airplane while Billy Idol says "Aw right!"

But what happens when the plane lands? What happens when the excitement dies down and they find themselves engaging in mundane tasks like shopping for groceries and unclogging gutters? Will they fight a lot? Will they discover that they don't have much in common? Will they wind up cheating on each other in an effort to recreate the thrill of a first kiss? We'll never know, because these are the ques-tions that Hollywood likes to avoid. The kaboom moment is all we crave, and the answer to the question "Now what?" rarely makes the final cut.

A couple of days after my own personal kaboom, the stu-pid smile became a furrowed brow as I asked myself the same question. Incidentally, "Now what?" is the question I spelled out in white tape on my graduation cap during com-mencement ceremonies at UMass. The band was playing, proud parents were snapping pictures, champagne corks were flying dangerously close to my eyes, and I didn't have a clue where to go or what to do.

I was scared and excited then, and I was scared and excited now. I could have dealt with the "fear" part by blam-ing the ethereal experience on nothing more than wishful thinking, or a spate of well-deserved, temporary insanity. Then I could have gone back to my safe, predictable, and clearly defined life. I could have told myself that I was too damn busy to be bothered with a spiritual awakening; after all, I had a stressful career to worry about.

I could have dealt with the "excitement" part by whipping myself into a spiritual frenzy while trying desperately to recreate the kaboom. I could've focused entirely on the event itself, viewing it as a means to an end, the final chapter as opposed to the starting point. And had it not been for my Buddhist training, I might have done just that.

Back in days when I was fidgeting and fussing on the meditation mat, I read that the most fruitful meditation experience can actually become a burden. If one catches a glimpse of the Divine while sitting in the lotus position, he or she should be grateful and use the experience to deepen his or her practice. But one shouldn't lust after it, or fantasize about tasting the Divine each time the meditation mat is rolled out. If this happens, the practice will become frustrating, and one's meditation routine will ultimately come to an end. Thus, while the moment in which God spoke to me was utterly amazing unto itself, I understood that it was not something to which I should cling. If I spent a great deal of time hoping to conjure up similar experiences at the drop of a hat, I would be sorely disappointed.

No, what occurred that afternoon had been a gift, a rare and precious gift of which I most certainly felt unworthy. Therefore, I had a responsibility not to squander it. Unfortunately, spiritual awakenings don't come with an instruction manual.

7 *Karen Favreau*

A.D.

8

No Words

During those times in my life when I've felt intrigued, curious, puzzled and/or befuddled, I've almost always sought out books. For example, when I was ten years old I decided that it would behoove me to learn about NFL football. Even though everyone in my family detested sports, I wanted to understand more about the shoulder pad-clad behemoths who chased after a funny-shaped ball every Sunday. Thanks to a book called *Football Talk* from the public library, I was able to decipher the mysteries of first downs, penalties, blitzes, free safeties, and onside kicks; within weeks, a lifelong affinity was born. Books would go on to guide me through my obsessions with the Beatles, country music, Libertarianism, and Buddhism. And without books, my current understanding of Christianity would be flimsy at best.

Nancy Malone, author of *Walking a Literary Labyrinth: A Spirituality of Reading,* believes that reading is inextricably linked to spiritual and personal growth. She writes:

> That is why I read, I guess, to stay alive, to be as fully alive as I can be. In books, almost the whole world and everything in it are available to me to feed that life. The words we usually use to name that appetite—*interest, curiosity*—aren't good enough to describe the impulse, and *pleasure*

doesn't adequately describe its satisfaction.
It is the need to know and understand—myself,
others, the world beyond me, God—to ask
about what is real and true and good and of
value, about how we should live our lives.

I couldn't agree more.

If every journey commences with a single step, mine led me straight into Borders. I fondled new CDs and flipped through rock 'n' roll magazines for a while before mustering up enough courage to saunter over to the "Christianity" section; I prayed that no one would recognize me. I had no clue where to start but knew instinctively what to avoid. I quickly dismissed the scary apocalyptic books along with the heavy tomes on theology. I passed over anything with sappy cover pictures of doves, mountains, or smiling children as well.

And then I saw it: *Finding Your Religion* by Unitarian minister Scotty McLennan. Not only was the title apropos of my current situation, but it also featured cover art courtesy of *Doonesbury* creator Gary Trudeau.

I bought the book.

I found Reverend McLennan's writing style to be down-to-earth, accessible, and not the least bit preachy. He begins by equating one's spiritual journey with the act of climbing a mountain, a not-too-original metaphor that worked just fine for me at the time. Before preparing to scale the heights and take in the gorgeous view at the top, however, McLennan urges us to choose one clearly marked path.

I recalled reading something similar by Buddhist author Jack Kornfield in which he'd urged new seekers to settle into the rhythms of one well-worn religious tradition, an act he defined as "choosing one seat." Jumping from one practice to another as soon as the novelty wears off never allows the practitioner to face his or her boredom, doubts, and fears; spirituality becomes all about the thrill of the chase rather than growth.

I could see their point. After all, the religion soup I'd stirred up had done little to quell my hunger.

Upon choosing a path, McLennan assures us that it's okay to "change seats" if, after having given the practice more than a fair shake, you discover that it's not getting you where you need to be. This was exactly what I needed to hear. Perfectionist that I am, I'd felt like a failure for aborting my Buddhist journey short of attaining Nirvana. But now I was learning that it's okay to stumble and start again, and that here are many ways to reach the summit.

McLennan goes on to stress the importance of traveling with companions, preferably older and wiser folks who'd "been there and done that." He writes:

> It is my experience, though, that the spiritual mountain is best climbed along marked trails and paths. Of course, it's possible to make progress by striking out on one's own and bushwhacking through the brambles and undergrowth. That may also seem a lot more exhilarating and much more fun—for a while, anyway. It's also a lot easier that way to get lost, exhausted, and burned out. This can be lonely and frightening if you're by yourself.

I remembered how lonely I'd felt when trying to study the Dharma without the aid of friends with whom to discuss the dense and confusing doctrine. I thought about books with titles like *Wicca for the Solitary Practitioner*, books that encourage the reader to fly solo and create his or her own path without embracing the knowledge of those who had stumbled to salvation before them. I knew enough about myself to recognize that if I tried scaling the heights alone, I'd probably get bored and switch to a new extreme sport, despite having spent far too much money on hiking boots, pulleys, and protein bars.

And then I remembered that I hated groups.

In the early nineties, one-hit-wonder band Blind Melon put out a memorable video for the song "No Rain." It featured a chubby, bespectacled girl in a bee costume who wandered around town in search of fellow bees with whom she could fraternize. Right as she appeared to be teetering on the verge of despair, bee-girl wandered into a bucolic field filled with bee-people of all ages, shapes, and sizes who were frolicking in the flowers, completely secure in their identity. The story ends with bee-girl rushing toward her new family and joining in the festivities without missing a beat.

I loved that video because I could identify with the bee-girl's quest. I'd spent most of my adult life searching for a group of people who would embrace me and infuse my life with meaning. But each time, I walked away from the groups empty, disillusioned, and bitter. This was also how I felt after buying the Blind Melon CD and finding that "No Rain" was the only decent song on it.

Would Christians turn out to be one more group of people who let me down?

So I began to pray for guidance. My first attempts at talking to God were awkward and stilted in the way that conversations with people we've hurt in the past tend to be.

"Um . . . God . . . I'm sorry about that time I called Christianity the *opium of the masses*. Nothing personal . . . I was drunk. Can we be friends again?"

Then, as the formality subsided and I became more comfortable with this new task, I found myself bursting into tears as soon as my knees hit carpet. I was overwhelmed by the enormity of the fact that God had not abandoned me. I was filled with gratitude, *bursting* with gratitude, thrilled to have had this mysterious gift of faith bestowed upon me.

And I cried because each time I kneeled beside my bed I felt completely naked, my thoughts and desires laid out before God without the illusory protection provided by my guitar, my cynicism, and that black leather biker jacket I'd purchased in New York. God didn't care that I had a master's degree. He didn't care about my portfolio of published cartoons, or the fact that I had a pretty damn good CD collection. He knew when I was exaggerating, and when I was holding back.

I was reluctant to share my intense and often overwhelming feelings with those friends and family members who knew all too well about my string of obsessions. If I revealed the details of my awakening and newfound faith, would they roll their eyes and act as though they'd received an invitation to my fifth wedding ceremony?

For the next three months, I wrestled with a mystery illness and watched helplessly as my weight plummeted. When I'd put the booze away five years before, the pounds had dropped abruptly from the cessation of empty calories. Despite eating generous quantities of food wherever and whenever I felt like it, I never gained those pounds back.

As a result, I was subjected to the inquiries of complete strangers who wished to learn the secret behind my sleek physique. Since phrases like "self-control," "low-carb," and "calorie counting" weren't in my vocabulary, I'd usually respond with something like, "Oh, it's just genetic." When I dared complain about my inability to gain weight, people would dismiss me with the declaration, "You just have high metabolism," before adding, "If I could only be so lucky!"

My gastroenterologist poked, prodded, and tested me for every disorder known to humankind, and every test came back negative. We ruled out Crohn's Disease, cancer, thyroid disorders, parasites, tapeworms, and kinks in my colon. I peed in a orange plastic pitcher, swallowed barium, popped pills, and gathered my bowel movements in small sterile cups. Meanwhile, my illness remained undiagnosed.

Throughout it all, I tried my best to keep a sense of humor, albeit a sardonic one. I told friends and co-workers that I was auditioning for a role as a heroin-addicted Holocaust victim.

"Mr. Spielberg, I'm ready for my close up," I'd say while trying not to pass out and hit the floor, terrified that I would wind up back in the operating room.

I had two choices at that point. The first was to do exactly what I'd done when my intestines stopped working twenty years before, which was tell God to take a hike. The second choice involved embracing God and asking him to comfort me while I suffered.

I chose the latter.

Had I not spent two years reading Buddhist theology, I might not have been able to make the decision so easily. When it comes to suffering, the Buddhists are harsh realists. Instead of denying suffering, they urge us to embrace it, acknowledge it, and learn from it. But for many of us raised

Christian, especially those of us who never delved beyond the fluffy stuff we learned as kids in Sunday school, suffering is something we can try to bargain away, and prayer the means by which we bargain. We say things like, "God, if you let me get this job, then I'll start going to church every week," or "Dear Lord, if you just help me get out of this mess, then I'll never cheat on my wife again." And so on.

No, when I made the decision to ride out the pain with God by my side, I began praying for *strength* rather than for stuff. I prayed that my faith would not wane in the face of my illness. I prayed that I would have the courage to accept whatever diagnosis came my way, no matter how much it scared me. And I prayed that I would learn from my experience, much as St. Ignatius had done when he broke his leg after being thrown from a horse in battle. Rather than bitch and moan about the fate that had befallen him, Ignatius spent his recuperative period pondering the mysteries of God and praying for wisdom and clarity. And when he recovered, kaboom, he invented the Jesuits. Talk about making lemonade from lemons.

"Let your will, not my own, be done," I'd pray, my hands clenched tightly, my brain not always believing the words coming from my mouth.

Throughout the whole ordeal, I continued to drag myself to work, play the occasional gig, and attend Mass at St. Agatha's. But the folks there weren't very friendly. Even though I sat in the same pew every Saturday night, nobody ever bothered to introduce themselves or say, "Welcome to St. Agatha's." With all of the bad press the Catholic Church had been receiving at that point, one would think that priests and parishioners all over the country would be rolling out red carpets and offering toaster ovens to each new person who walked through the door. So I continued to read about the Protestants.

During my lunch hour one Friday, I consulted the Internet for information about churches in the Greensboro area. I plugged search terms such as "Presbyterian + Greensboro" and "Methodist + Guilford County," into Yahoo, but nothing came up that made me want to jump out of my chair. Then I entered "Episcopalian + Greensboro," and was directed to the website for St. Andrew's Episcopal Church. The site's background was pink. The text clearly stated that everyone was welcome. And it featured a photo of a female priest with short white hair smiling broadly and looking as happy as a clam to be spreading the Good News.

"This is it," I mumbled to myself between bites of an egg-salad sandwich. "This is the church I'm supposed to join."

Maybe it was the hot-pink background, or the fact that, after years of hanging out in Catholicism's "No Girls Allowed" club, the sight of a female in flowing priestly robes struck me as something pretty damn incredible. I had asked God to lead me to a loving church, and I had a feeling that my prayers had been answered; all that was missing was a rousing rendition of Handel's "Hallelujah Chorus."

The next day, I e-mailed the woman in the picture, even though the only thing I knew about Episcopalianism was that the word has far too many syllables.

9

Go Tell it on the Mountain

During a recent spate of nostalgia, I dug out a pile of albums from the 1980s and hooked up my turntable. As I dropped the needle on Adam and the Ants' *Prince Charming* LP, I closed my eyes and recalled the poster of a sexy, shirtless Adam Ant in leather pants that hung on my door as a teenager. By the second verse of "Stand and Deliver," however, I said, "What is this crap?" and lifted the needle from the vinyl. The same thing happened when I tried to muddle through Wham's *Make It Big* album in its entirety. Granted, "Careless Whisper" has aged surprisingly well, but listening to the other songs was nothing short of torture.

The fact that these records did not move me in any profound manner is a good thing, because it proved that my musical horizons have expanded. There are still some people my age who would name Journey's *Escape* as the greatest album of all time, but, for the most part, our tastes in music, literature, and lovers evolve as we're faced with new challenges and experiences. Can you imagine going to a party and stating, without a hint of sarcasm in your voice, that *The Facts of Life* is a brilliant sitcom, or that *Footloose* is the pinnacle of cinematic accomplishment?

Yet, when it comes to spirituality, many of us are content to base our current religious beliefs on those things we learned at the wise old age of sixteen. I had not taken the time to revaluate the teachings and tenets of my childhood faith before making sweeping derogatory statements about Christianity in my twenties. It did not occur to me that my interpretation of scripture and theology should change as my world got bigger and my ideas got broader. I was content to rest on the assumption that, since I found church and sermons boring as a restless and immature sixteen-year-old, I would find them boring as a more stable adult. Like many of my peers, my spiritual maturity remained stunted, while my emotional maturity evolved.

These were some of the ideas running through my head as I rang the buzzer at St. Andrew's Episcopal Church.

If Reverend Z. was caught off-guard by my sunken cheekbones and baggy clothing, she did a very good job of hiding her surprise. Or maybe she thought that I was a former crack-head who'd finally seen the light. Regardless, she listened patiently while I related the tale of my Catholic upbringing, my drunken atheist days, my conversion experience, and my current illness. We moved onto the subject of books, and I discovered that Reverend Z. was also a passionate bibliophile.

As the hour wound down, she assured me that everyone was welcome at St. Andrew's, and that dissenting opinion and lively debate regarding theology's big questions were encouraged. She went on to explain that, in addition to Scripture and tradition, the Episcopal Church prides itself on embracing rational thought. For a gal who once placed all of her eggs in Ayn Rand's Objectivist basket, the church's emphasis on reason and spirited discourse were very strong selling points indeed.

I decided to give the Episcopal Church a shot.

As I sat through my first service at St. Andrew's the following week, I noted that it was remarkably similar to the Catholic Mass in terms of liturgical structure and "pew aerobics" (sit, stand, kneel, repeat). We shook hands during the peace offering, listened to three Scripture readings, and received absolution for our sins. The style of dress, however, was a bit more formal than I had anticipated. Awash in a sea of pearls, neckties, and floral-print dresses, I regretted having worn jeans.

When the congregants gathered in line for Communion, I remained seated in deference to my "intruder" status. Because the Catholic Church was very clear in its teaching that only baptized Catholics can partake in the Eucharist, I assumed that all denominations played by such stringent rules.

"Everyone is welcome to join in Communion," Reverend Z. later explained. "Jesus didn't turn anyone away, and neither do we."

So there was no secret handshake or mysterious password after all.

Determined to stick with "one seat," but worried that my fervor might wane after a while, I told the Reverend that I wanted to get involved in some sort of committee right off the bat. She suggested that I plug into the Stewardship Team, which was meeting later that week at a local restaurant.

With my head still firmly planted in the clouds, I was half-expecting to find a table full of people holding hands and singing "Kumbaya" when I walked into the restaurant. Instead, I encountered a group of perfectly normal people drinking cocktails and gossiping. After years of arduously avoiding all things alcohol, here I was surrounded by booze at my very first church function; the Creator certainly has a twisted sense of humor.

The dinner meeting was a mix of business and pleasure. God's name did not come up, except during the obligatory prayer at the end. I was so eager to share my conversion experience with someone, so desperate to engage in some heavy God talk, that I thought I would burst. But I acted politely, joined in the small talk, and avoided bringing up the G-word altogether.

I refer to my first few months at St. Andrew's as my "embarrassingly sincere" stage, a period in which I wanted nothing more than to climb up on the roof and testify to the healing power of God's mercy. I somehow managed to refrain from discussing my spiritual quest with cashiers and post office clerks, regardless of the fact that my ravenous hunger was growing deeper and deeper.

Incidentally, I wrote the following journal entry around that time:

When I started this journal three years ago,
I went from focusing on Buddhism to animal
rights and vegetarianism to an obsession with
therapy to becoming a Christian. No wonder
I'm always so tired . . .

0   0   0

Thanks to a Catholic background in which priests were viewed as holier than the average schmuck, I came to St. Andrew's assuming that Reverend Z.'s prayers somehow carried more weight than those of the laity. I also viewed her as my own personal direct link to God. Let's face it, if God had deigned to speak to someone as lowly as me, then he and the Reverend Z. probably spoke on the phone every Wednesday night.

I suppose that, regardless of one's denomination, we tend to transform priests and ministers into one-dimensional caricatures based on our needs and individual weaknesses. For those fragile, lonely individuals who wander into church, the person on the altar can quickly become a substitute mommy or daddy. For someone seeking a solution to all of their woes, this one-dimensional pillar of holiness can become a sort of shaman in their eyes. Unrealistic expectations about what the man or woman with collar can do for you are par for the course.

Back in my days at the homeless shelter, the clients often ended their tales of drunken debauchery with the phrase "But you wouldn't know about that." They never bothered to ask me if I'd experimented with drugs and alcohol because, to the broken men and women, it was important that I remain a symbol of uncorrupted innocence. While their assumption of my "purity" made me laugh, I suppose that the illusion was necessary. Had I stuck around longer, I would have felt compelled to shatter it.

I personally wasn't looking for a mommy or a magician, but I was looking for answers to my myriad questions regarding God. If Reverend Z. made a suggestion, I took it. If she mentioned a book, I ran out and read it, and then tried to wow her with my wit and insight. I found myself playing "Impress the pastor," much as I once played "Impress the guitar teacher" with my rock 'n' roll mentor Doug Hewitt.

If my early attempts at learning to play the guitar were predicated on getting my teacher to like me, it didn't take long for the sheer joy of creating music to become a reward unto itself. I can still recall the night when, too wired to sleep, I wandered out of my dorm room with my guitar and proceeded to strum it. Within minutes, a crowd of drunken music lovers spilled into the hallway for what turned into a spontaneous sing-a-long of Pink Floyd's "Wish You Were Here." The moment was glorious, and I didn't once think about Doug. Nor did I think about him when I wowed a cocky guitar goon with a flawless rendition of the first few measures of "Stairway to Heaven."

Likewise, by sticking with "one seat" and facing my fears, prejudices, and projections, I was allowed to rediscover Reverend Z. as a flawed but very wonderful *human being.* As I got more comfortable in my new Episcopalian identity and removed the rose-colored glasses I'd so eagerly donned, I learned that we're *all* ministers of God's word, and that a collar doesn't guarantee the wearer a one-way ticket to paradise.

Eventually, my desire to "Impress the pastor" would wane, and I attended services and read voraciously about the Christian faith simply because doing so fed my soul. If my church attendance was consistent, it was not because I wanted a gold star and a cookie from the church elders.

How exhausting it must be to carry the hopes and desires of an entire congregation. Thank you, Reverend Z., for your patience during my embarrassingly sincere days at St. Andrew's. And thank you for your humanity.

"How do you talk about God?"

This was the question posed by a Southern Baptist acquaintance of mine after I informed her of my new status as a Christian. I was stunned to hear the question come out of her mouth; after all, isn't that what Southern Baptists *do*? Don't they talk about God until your ears bleed?

Of course, "talking" and "communicating" are not the same thing. Shouting from the rooftops may get people's attention, but it might not be the best way to convey a message. I asked Cheri, a fellow congregant at St. Andy's, why people seem to be so reluctant to engage in emotional discussions about their spiritual paths during coffee hour.

"For some people, faith is just too personal," she replied.

But I *wanted* to wear my faith on my sleeve . . . and my bumper . . . and, come to think of it, my wall, my mouse pad, and my coffee mug. Let's face it, upon discovering a particularly interesting rock band, movie, restaurant, or novel, I'm inclined to rave about the phenomenon to anyone within earshot. I am not shy about my politics or my penchant for vegetarian cuisine; in fact, my enthusiastic endorsement of soymilk has resulted in no less than four acquaintances swearing off dairy products forever. Yet, I dared not breach the boundaries of social etiquette by tooting my Christian horn too loudly; didn't Emily Post teach us that discussing religion in polite company was tacky?

Concerns about etiquette aside, I was also faced with the dilemma of how to share my new faith with my wonderful atheist and agnostic acquaintances. I'd spent years assembling a tight circle of friends who were antagonistic to organized religion, friends with whom I'd spent countless hours making fun of televangelists, "Virgin Mary-in-a-half-shell" lawn ornaments, and Anita Bryant. How would they react to the news that their former drinking buddy had found Jesus?

It took a few weeks, but I finally mustered up enough courage to "come out" as a Christian. Unfortunately, those friends of mine who would never think of discriminating against someone because of skin color, sexual preference, or country of origin were less than enthused about my news.

"Please respect my stance as an atheist, and don't preach to me," was the blunt response of a loved one. "Whatever gets you through the night," was the blasé reply of another. And when my dear friend Sara and her husband came to visit, the simple statement "I've started going back to church, and I'm very happy as a Christian" was met with a silence so thick and deadly that I thought we'd all suffocate.

My acquaintance Annie was a bit more animated. I told her about my awakening, and how some things just started to "make sense" as a result. I went on to explain that I'd tossed out my CDs by shock-rocker Marilyn Manson and bad-boy rapper Eminem in an effort to eliminate negativity from my life.

"I still like Eminem . . . do you think that's bad? Are you judging me? Are you judging me right now?"

I was taken aback by her defensive response, until I understood that she was genuinely curious to find out if my spiritual plunge had completely transformed my personality; besides, inquiry was better than silence.

"No, not at all," I explained. "Doing so was more of a symbolic gesture. I just feel that it's hypocritical of me to claim that I subscribe to the teachings of Jesus while simultaneously supporting a hatemonger like Eminem."

The exchange made me realize a couple of things. First, Christians have a terrible reputation for being "judgmental." Second, Emily Post knew what she was talking about.

We had barely crossed the Eminem hurdle when I made another statement that didn't sit well with Annie. This time the subject was Elvis. Because I am such a fan of the King, I've always been saddened by the fact that Elvis Presley's "friends" did not exercise the kind of tough love he so sorely needed as he spiraled into drug addiction. Having just bought an *Elvis Sings Gospel* CD, I remarked that, had he stuck with singing religious music, maybe he'd be alive today.

"Oh, so are Christians perfect or something?"

In Annie's eyes, I guess I was acting like a giddy, love-sick schoolgirl who'd found herself knee-deep in amorous intoxication. Dazzled by Jesus, the new man in my life, I'd torn up the photos of my ex-lovers and tossed them over the balcony with enviable drama-queen flair.

I did not bring up God for the rest of the night.

@ @ @

In a last-ditch attempt to pinpoint the cause of my illness, I underwent an endoscopy procedure. While poking around my digestive tract, the doctor discovered that the defective portion of duodenum that had been widened twenty years prior had become, in effect, "too wide." Without delving into unnecessarily gory details, suffice it to say that, when food

reached the damaged section, it sat around for a while in a little stagnant pool before sloshing along on the rest of its journey. Stagnant pools attract bacteria, and bacteria eat food, which explains why I'd been so hopelessly thin all those years. I'd managed to coexist somewhat peaceably with the microscopic marauders for a number of years, until all hell broke loose. Then my intestines could no longer juggle my needs with theirs.

The good news was that I would not need surgery. The bad news, which could have been worse, was that I would need to take antibiotics for the rest of my life. I quickly developed an affinity for yogurt.

Within a few months, I would gain more than twenty pounds. I heard the phrase "Karen, you look so . . . *healthy*" at least once a day as flesh and color returned to my once-sunken cheeks. Yes, riding shotgun with God had made the journey less frightening, and I thanked him profusely when the bumpy ride was over. Had he "tested" me as I'd proclaimed weeks before? Was I a modern-day Job, an unwilling participant in a sick contest between God and the Prince of Darkness? I highly doubt it, as I just can't believe that God wills human suffering. I do, however, believe that God can help us redeem it.

With my ability to properly digest food restored, I was free to exert more energy on spiritual matters. Yet, as much as I felt myself drawn to St. Andrew's, my long-standing hatred for groups flared up again and again. I was the new kid on the block, and, at times, I felt as though I were back in the high school cafeteria, lunch tray in hand, surveying the room in search of a familiar face. I prayed that my insecurity and painful shyness would not sabotage my attempts at finding community.

Despite the testimonials of many a born-again Christian, I can assure you that embracing Jesus did not magically eliminate my shyness and painful insecurity. The folks at St. Andrew's were incredibly welcoming and did their best to make me feel at home; but, for us shy Christians, the fundamental group dynamics at a church aren't much different from that of a bowling league or sewing circle. While we were all at St. Andrew's based on a profound desire to praise God and find meaning in our lives, it would take me a while to find peers with whom I truly clicked.

On those Sundays when I felt completely invisible at coffee hour, the enticing "Why do I need to go to church to be a Christian?" question would creep into my thoughts. Luckily, this dilemma was addressed in a sermon that I desperately needed to hear, a phenomenon that seemed to happen frequently. Reverend Z. stated from the pulpit that Christianity is *not* a loner religion. Jesus didn't appear to his disciples on a one-on-one basis after the Resurrection. Rather, He chose to speak to the whole gaggle of them, that sprawling, imperfect, dysfunctional family of followers in whom he entrusted his message. Why? Because that was the only way it was going to work.

Like it or not, I needed to immerse myself in that sprawling, imperfect, dysfunctional family at St. Andrew's. So I forced myself to return to Scotty McLellan's metaphorical mountain again and again in those shy and shaky days. I recognized that the sermons I heard, the prayer meetings I attended, and the weekly worship services in which I participated were lighting the path and leading me to the summit. If I ran out of trail mix and bottled water along the way, somebody would be there to lend me some. And maybe, at some point, I'd be able to return the favor.

Trying to grasp the enormity of God's message alone is a bit like attempting to read *Beowulf* without the aid of a patient English professor or a copy of Cliff Notes. If we try to understand the mystery that is God all by ourselves, then we're no better off than the proverbial blind men and the elephant, each one erroneously convinced that he'd uncovered the true pachyderm paradigm.

I can still recall the amazement I felt in watching a group of church ladies spring into action faster than a NASCAR pit crew upon learning that a member of the congregation had undergone surgery. Cards were signed, people volunteered to cook meals for his family, and transportation accommodations were put into place so that the poor fellow would have a way to get to his doctor appointments upon returning home. Even though I had yet to delve deeply into the

Scriptures, I felt pretty sure that the church ladies were doing Jesus' work.

I discovered a piece by St. Teresa of Avila around this time that captured the notion of Christian interdependence quite nicely:

> Christ has no body now on earth but yours;
> Yours are the only hands with which he can do
>   his work
> Yours are the only feet with which he can go
>   about the world
> Yours are the only eyes through which his com-
>   passion can shine forth
> upon a troubled world
> Christ has no body now on earth but yours.

I supposed that, by calling myself a Christian, I had an implicit duty to act as Jesus' hands, feet, and eyes. Yet, loving my neighbors, sharing my bounty, visiting the sick and treating all people, no matter how obnoxious, as children of God, sounded like pretty difficult stuff; would I really be able to pull it off? By calling myself a Christian, the bar had been raised, and slapping a St. Andrew's sticker on the back of my Honda would no longer be sufficient. How on earth could I have ever called Christianity an opiate? Opium encourages passivity. Christianity promotes action.

But let's get back to that sticker for a moment. While displaying the St. Andrew's logo on my rear windshield didn't make me holier than the average driver, it *did* make me think twice before flipping off fellow motorists. The Lord works in mysterious ways.

10

Sin City

"God loves everyone equally."

Reverend Z. said these words as I left her office and headed toward my car. When I pulled out of the parking lot, they began to weigh heavily upon me.

"God loves everyone equally."

On the surface, it was a beautiful sentiment. And yet, the four little words bothered me. They sat there like a hangnail begging to be picked, until I could take it no more.

"But . . . but . . . *that's not fair*!"

No one was there to hear my response, but I repeated it anyway.

"But that's not fair."

If God loves everyone equally, then why was I wasting my time going to church, reading books, pondering life's big questions, and trying to be nice to people? If God loved me as a drunk, then why not pick up a six-pack on the way home and proceed to get wasted? If God loved me as an angry atheist, then why struggle with the challenges of faith?

As I continued the drive home, it occurred to me that the religious lessons I'd learned as a child were beginning to poke through the soil. Let's face it, the version of Catholicism that I remembered was *all about* fairness. If you followed the Commandments and the teachings of the One True Church, you went to heaven; those who violated the teachings did not. Why? Because fair is fair. Un-baptized babies didn't get to spend eternity with God. Why? Because it wouldn't be fair to all those kiddies in the little white gowns whose parents had followed the law to the letter. And so on.

My old Catholic teachings would bump up against the Episcopal Church's more liberal theology when I started Confirmation class in the Fall. Upon hearing that all of God's children are saved on account of Jesus Christ's death and resurrection, I raised my hand and asked the speaker to repeat himself; surely I'd misunderstood. Once again, I found myself struggling with the whole notion of fairness. I thought back to those pagan babies, the ones we'd desperately wanted to rescue, and, for a moment, I missed the sense of urgency that I'd felt back then. "No baptism, no kingdom of God," was what we'd been taught. Would I have been motivated to sacrifice baseball card money if I'd been told that the heathens were all going to the same place that we pious Catholics were headed?

It wasn't until I began to contemplate the Episcopal Church's teaching on "sin" that it all started to make sense. Unlike some denominations that take pleasure in creating long lists of actions that qualify as sin, Episcopalians define the term simply as "a separation from God." Of course, this raises the question "So how do you know if you're sinning?" I believe that Supreme Court Justice Potter Stewart answered the question best when he attempted to define pornography: "You know it when you see it."

Yes, we just know. When we engage in cruel, selfish, or ugly actions, God's absence is palpable.

So why was I getting so hung up about "fairness"? Was I really so competitive and selfish that I wanted God's love all to myself? And where did this whole concept of "fairness" to which I subscribed come from anyway? According to anthropologists at Emory University, a sense of fairness evolved long before humans did. I read about a study they conducted in which five capuchin monkeys were taught to exchange a small stone token for a slice of cucumber. One token, one slice. Then the researchers changed the rules and began giving some of the monkeys more food for their tokens. The "one slice" monkeys got peeved and refused to play along unless better food options emerged; some even threw the proffered cucumber across the cage in disgust. The researchers concluded that monkeys have an innate notion of justice that allows them to live cooperatively.

So how are we supposed to transcend this supposed innate sense of justice? How are we supposed to feel content with a lousy cucumber slice when less deserving humans are walking around with lasagna and lobster? I suppose it's because God has enough love to go around, period. After all, despite the nasty things I'd said about him, God took me back without a second thought. On that warm February afternoon, for one glorious, fleeting moment, I felt the whole of God's love wash over me. Did I deserve it? Hell, no.

But let's get back to sin for a moment, as it's gotten a pretty bad rap in recent years. Talk show hosts and twelve-steppers denounce it as an outdated and mean-spirited concept that only hinders spiritual growth. But if we look at sin as separation from God, then I'm convinced that we need to be talking about it even more. This is not because I think that sinners will burn in Hell, their flesh falling off in bloody chunks, their bones ground to dust beneath the hooves of Lucifer. No, we need to talk about sin because separation from God is the loneliest feeling we will ever know.

0   0   0

In addition to the Anglican definition of sin, my Confirmation classes taught me that I wasn't the only member of St. Andrew's who'd become an Episcopalian via a circuitous route. Every week, I sat side-by-side with folks who'd grown up Catholic, Presbyterian, Methodist, and Baptist, each of us carrying some form of spiritual baggage from our previous journeys. So, in light of the teachings of my adopted denomination, the question "How much baggage should I leave at the door, and how much should I lug down the aisles?" is one that I began to ponder.

Could I be a good Episcopalian by sitting in the lotus position when I prayed rather than getting on my knees? Did the fact that I declined to partake in the wine offering at church make me less of an Anglican? Was it okay that I sort of missed seeing Jesus on the crucifix instead of those clean, empty, *Protestant* crosses?

"Karen, when you broaden and deepen your faith, you don't tear down or toss out your foundation," was the sensible reply of my friend Julie, a fellow Catholic-turned-Episcopalian.

Recently, I met an amazing woman at the library named Sharon who told me a story that put these "baggage" worries to rest once and for all. Sharon, who'd struggled with undiagnosed dyslexia for years, did not learn to read and write until she was fifty-two years old. As a result, she'd devised ingenious coping strategies to hide this dark secret from friends, co-workers, and family members. For example, because she couldn't read a menu, Sharon would always order one of the specials rattled off by the waiter when dining out with friends. And when wrapping birthday or Christmas presents, she'd attach a fresh flower to the package in lieu of a gift tag.

During her first Christmas as an adult reader, Sharon ditched the flowers and placed traditional cards and tags on her carefully wrapped gifts. Convinced that these were far superior to her previous method of self-identification, she was shocked to hear a friend ask, "Where's the flower?" upon receiving her present.

"There's a card on there that I wrote!"

"I don't want a card. Everybody does cards!" was the friend's reply. "There's nothing special about that. You just go back to using flowers."

So Sharon has reclaimed the practice of garnishing her gifts with back-eyed Susans and daisies.

"We need to grow," she says. "But, there are things about us that are good the way they were, so I'm not going to change everything."

So I continue to sit in the lotus position when I pray. I'll always prefer folk music to choral music, and I'll never lose my fascination with the saints or incense. There are probably some men and women at St. Andrew's who pray to the Virgin Mary, some who meditate and chant, and some who think ten-minute sermons are much too short. Regardless, we all sidle up to the altar rail come Sunday, each of us with our unique baggage, some of us bearing gift tags and some of us bearing flowers. And we're all richer because of it.

As the scales of ignorance were dropping from my eyes, my duo was falling apart. I suppose that Shannon and I simply had different expectations of what it meant to be part of a duo. I expected her to rehearse religiously and pound the pavement in search of lucrative gigs, while she expected me to be less of a control freak. I think this is what they call "artistic differences" in the music business.

Okay, maybe I can be a bit of a control freak regarding the creative process, but, unless someone assumes the role of leader in a band, nothing will ever get done. This was the problem Gene Simmons encountered in KISS. Despite working his fire-breathing butt off to make KISS insanely popular, guitarist Ace Frehley and drummer Peter Criss resented Gene's work ethic, and quit the band. Granted, having to put up with someone as annoying as Gene Simmons on a regular basis might be a bit challenging, but one does have to respect the sacrifices he made to ensure that the KISS logo became as ubiquitous as that of Nike.

But I digress . . .

Did the fact that I'd embraced a religion that Shannon had rejected have anything to do with our VH1 *Behind the Music*-worthy breakup? Perhaps. Regardless, after a bitter e-mail exchange in which nasty things were furiously typed by both parties, we called it quits. I was devastated and very, very angry. Because making music is such an intense and deeply personal phenomenon, the emotions involved in the dissolution of a rock band often rival those experienced at the end of a romantic relationship.

It was time to learn a little lesson about forgiveness. Instead of returning to the metaphorical mountain this time around, I returned to Anne Lamott's *Traveling Mercies*, specifically the line that read: "Not forgiving is like drinking rat poison and then waiting for the rat to die." What a glorious image! Holding grudges, grumbling, and fantasizing about cruel and unusual punishment do nothing to kill the rat. While he's happily spreading plague and pestilence, we're allowing anger to eat away at us from the inside out.

Oh, but it's so much easier to forgive in *theory* than in *practice,* just like it's easier to love "humanity" as opposed to that one annoying relative or library customer whose mere existence causes my jaw to clench and my neck muscles to tighten. Conversion experiences do not wash the recipient clean of petty insecurities, bad habits, or a proclivity for holding grudges. No, the convert must first want to rid himself of these things, and then pray like mad for the strength to follow through. I got into the habit of attaching "with your help" to my prayers, as in "with your help, may I stop fantasizing about Shannon accidentally stepping on her guitar and then crashing through the screen door. Amen."

And then, with God's help, I began praying *for* her. Let's face it, I didn't hate Shannon, I was just angry that things hadn't gone my way. I reminded myself that, because of our short-lived duo, I'd been forced to tackle challenging songs, thus becoming a better guitar player. I gained some valuable studio experience and was exposed to a number of interesting artists I might not have otherwise discovered. Not that I would ever admit this to her. . . .

Shannon, may you keep on singing, and eventually find someone with whom you click musically. May you belt out tunes for the heck of it, and never lose your passion for the perfect pop song. And most important, may you find happiness. With God's help, of course.

———— ◆ ————

Because I was only one of many wayward sheep in need of the shepherd's attention, I asked Reverend Z. if she could hook me up with a "God Buddy." I was slowly letting my guard down at church, but still didn't feel close enough to any one congregant to bore him or her with lengthy ramblings about sin, salvation, and the advantages of praying in the lotus position versus on one's knees. I envisioned this God Buddy as a fellow Episcopalian with whom I'd feel comfortable engaging in deep theological discussions; this lucky soul would be privy to all of my profound and witty observations.

Reverend Z. suggested that I speak to a woman named Barbara who lived in my neighborhood. Despite the fact that Barbara was twenty-five years my senior, we hit it off, and began carpooling to church events. Shortly thereafter, Barbara went into the hospital for knee replacement surgery. The doctors told us that she'd be up and running in no time, but fate proved otherwise. Barbara went under the knife once again when her replacement knee became infected, and she found herself flat on her back for months like a modern-day St. Ignatius.

Needless to say, the God buddy plan didn't turn out as I'd envisioned. Instead of dissecting the Nicene Creed or discussing the finer points of intercessory prayer, I found myself visiting Barbara with McDonald's vanilla milkshakes and library books in tow. No, we didn't engage in a whole lot of theology talk during her ordeal, and I believe that this is probably a good thing.

Trying to impress people by dropping names and posing philosophical arguments is the *easy* part of Christianity. Visiting a sick person you don't know very well in a nursing home that reeks of urine is the *hard* part. Jesus didn't sit around in a cave reading the Old Testament all day. Granted, he was well acquainted with Scripture and quoted it a great deal, but he is mostly remembered for going out into the community and helping people. When he posed questions or challenged the Pharisees' interpretation of the law, it was not to prove how smart he was, but to change people's narrow view of the world.

So I got my head out of the books.

Self-absorbed person that I was, I found myself caught off guard by this nascent desire to do nice things for people like Barbara. And unlike those incidents in my childhood when I gave up stuff for Lent and refrained from taunting the unpopular, paste-eating kids because I thought doing so would get me into Heaven, I didn't have an agenda this time around. I no longer viewed God as someone who kept a "naughty and nice" ledger in which each action, good or bad, was recorded for future reference. I couldn't articulate what I was doing at the time, but I suppose that, instead of doing good deeds *to receive* God's grace, I was doing so *in response* to it.

Unfortunately, many religious people find themselves engaging in acts of kindness or refraining from acts of debauchery based on nothing more than a paralyzing fear of going to Hell. I'm guessing that these are the kinds of people who furtively place Chick tracts on the library shelves and under the windshield wipers of complete strangers' cars. I know you've encountered Chick tracts— they're those small, poorly drawn comic books in which characters who listen to rock 'n' roll, practice Catholicism, and celebrate Halloween end up begging for mercy in the afterlife beneath a cold, faceless God who banishes them to the fiery pit without a second thought. If Chick tracts weren't so despicable, they'd be pretty damn funny.

I hadn't engaged in any formal Bible study at that point, but I seemed to recall that Jesus is celebrated for the positive things he did during his short ministry. Had he spoke of nothing but fear and damnation, I doubt that Christianity would've lasted more than a generation or two. It was Jesus' love that attracted the multitudes, gave the outcasts hope and motivated sinners to reinvent themselves. And it was the message of love and acceptance I encountered at St. Andrew's that kept me coming back for more, even on those days when I tried to talk myself out of it.

This is not to say that "doing good" suddenly became easy, and that I walked around with a beatific aura around my body each and every day. I only have to flip through my journal entries to see that the "Christianity is hard" concept kept popping up in those early days.

> The conversion experience can be viewed as both a blessing and a burden. When we taste the Divine, we acknowledge that the rules have been changed. We recognize that many of the habits and infatuations of our everyday life are meaningless and absurd . . .
>
> Accepting Jesus Christ as a role model is quite ambitious . . .
>
> Following the example of Christ is not passive and it ain't easy. Issues regarding forgiveness

and acceptance are still tripping me up; if we forgive too easily, then the offender doesn't suffer. He gets his cake and eats it too. Yet, after years of offending God, he embraced me the moment I fell to my knees. Shouldn't I, with God's help, try to do the same?

Ah, back to that whole "but it's not fair" concept. I wrote the latter entry right around the time I learned that Episcopalians consider all of the deceased to be saints. I had reluctantly accepted the notion that God loves everyone equally, and that maybe, just maybe, everyone gets into Heaven. But calling everyone a "saint" was too much for this former Catholic schoolgirl to reconcile. In my mind, saints were those folks who chose to get their limbs lopped off rather than denounce Jesus Christ. They're women like Mother Teresa who spend their whole lives hugging lepers and cleaning their oozing wounds. Saints get burned at the stake and give all of their possessions away, period. Surely I didn't belong in their company.

I suppose that the saving grace of that last entry is the phrase "with God's help." In the time since I wrote those words, I have made peace with the Episcopal Church's inclusive theology regarding Heaven, saints, and God's love. But I didn't make peace with it on my own; I did so "with God's help." I did so because I prayed constantly for God to help me become less judgmental and more open-minded. It is a prayer I need to say every day because, right when I think I'm okay with the world, someone comes along and royally pisses me off, and the thought of God loving that person and greeting him or her at the pearly gates drives me crazy. So what do I do? I pray. And it's something I don't do nearly enough.

In case you're wondering, the "God Buddy" story has a happy ending. Barbara's knee finally healed, and she was able to return to work as a nurse's assistant. We continue to carpool to church events, and have become good friends who support each other when bad things happen. But most importantly, Barbara taught me that getting out and living life is ultimately more important than just pondering it, which is something I never would have learned from a hateful Chick tract.

11

Radical Compassion

After a few months of fumbling
and stumbling toward enlightenment, it occurred to me
that I'd yet to seriously crack open the Bible. Sure, I heard
snippets of Scripture every Sunday at church, but I hadn't
hunkered down with the Good Book for real. I owned a
copy and kept it on top of my bookcase for easy access, but
the thought of opening it up and trying to make sense of the
stories seemed too daunting a task.

"Where does one start?"

I asked my friend Ron this very same question when, for
no apparent reason, I decided to become an opera afi-
cionado.

"Do not start with the Germans," he warned me. "Try the
Italians; they're more user-friendly."

So rather than lending me Wagner's complete works, he
opted for *The Barber of Seville*. Good move, as I probably
would have been a bit overwhelmed by the trials and tribu-
lations of Tristan and Isolde.

Thus said, Reverend Z. suggested that I not start with the
Old Testament.

"Try the Gospels and Paul's letters," she suggested.
"They're more user-friendly."

So I signed up for a class on the Gospel of Luke. A journal
entry from this period captures my trepidation:

So I've found myself in a Bible study group. This phrase would've made me want to pound the crap out of myself less than a year ago. So why am I there? Because, aside from the stuff covered in the *Jesus Christ Superstar album* and the Book of Revelation passages quoted by Charles Manson during that whole Helter Skelter thing, I don't know squat about the Good Book.

I believe that, as a Christian, I have an obligation to know what I'm talking about. I mean, if I don a Miles Davis t-shirt, I will probably be approached by a rabid fan who'll wish to strike up a conversation about Miles' oeuvre. Since the only album of his I've ever listened to in its entirety is *Kind of Blue,* I wouldn't have much to contribute to the conversation. So why wear the shirt?

Yes, if I planned on continuing to toot my Christian horn, it would behoove me to peek at the Big Guy's play book. Besides, having a structured, regularly scheduled opportunity to think, talk, and argue about God meant that my faith was important enough for me to turn off the *Simpsons,* put on a jacket, and drive fifteen minutes down the road to church.

As someone who has had the joy of rediscovering the Bible as an adult, I would highly recommend that you read the Gospel of Luke in its entirety. If you don't have a Bible lying around your house, then check one out from the public library, borrow a copy from your Mom, or swipe one from the local Motel 6. If you're anything like me (God help you), you will be immediately struck by the fact that Jesus was, indeed, a pretty radical guy. And thanks to St. Andy's Bible study, I was able to learn the depth of Jesus' radical compassion.

Theologians have spent entire lifetimes contemplating the reasons Jesus came to this earth. While I'm still pretty new at this whole Christian thing, it's my understanding that one of the main reasons Jesus embarked upon his ministry was to reform Judaism. Jesus was a Jew, after all, and he was well versed in the teachings of the Old Testament. But he was also appalled at just how hung up his people had gotten about rules and regulations regarding "purity." Blood was considered impure, as were people who were sick or dying. Tax collectors were impure. Women were impure. Gentiles were *really* impure. Food needed to be prepared in a particular way, one's hands were to be washed in a specific manner, and no work could be done on the Sabbath. The scribes and Pharisees promoted the idea that, as long as you didn't go around eating pork, touching blood, or hanging out with lepers, then you could act like the biggest ass in the world and still be considered holy.

Thus, many of God's chosen people were more concerned with *avoiding* those things that were considered sinful than with *doing* things that would contribute to the betterment of society. I suppose it's easy to spend your life avoiding sin if you cloister yourself in a room and turn your back on the inherent messiness and turbulence of life. But, by doing so, you're also missing out on the chance to make a difference in the world.

I'm pretty sure that Whoopi Goldberg covered similar theological terrain in *Sister Act.*

But I digress . . .

The parable of the Good Samaritan perfectly illustrates the case of "avoiding sin vs. engaging in compassionate actions." While walking along the road, a man is attacked by brigands who beat him up and leave him for dead. Because contact with bodily fluids was considered impure, the priest and the Levite who come upon him cross the road and avert their gaze. By leaving the poor guy wallowing in a pool of his own blood, they had remained "holy."

And then, from out of nowhere, an "impure" Samaritan cleans the stranger's wounds, places him upon a donkey, and takes the man somewhere safe where he can recover and regain his strength. So by using this simple story, Jesus taught his followers that one's lineage, occupation, and self-designated "purity" are *not* important in the eyes of God. Rather, showing compassion for one's neighbor is the way into the kingdom of God. This was pretty radical stuff for 30 A.D.

As theologian Marcus Borg writes in *Meeting Jesus Again for the First Time*—a book recommended to me by, you guessed it, Reverend Z.: "We see the challenge to the purity system not only in Jesus' teaching but in many of his activities. The stories of his healings shatter the purity boundaries of his social world. He touched lepers and hemorrhaging women. He entered a graveyard inhabited by a man with a 'legion' of unclean spirits who lived in the vicinity of pigs, which were of course unclean animals."

Jesus also raised the ire of the local holy men by hanging out with tax collectors, hookers, and women in general, and by telling parables that highlighted the hypocrisy of the priests and Pharisees. Jesus went out of his way to prove that God loves all of his children, and that labels imposed by society are not recognized by the Creator.

After reading Luke, I could not comprehend how any Christian could study the Gospels and reach the conclusion that God withholds love from certain segments of society. I am especially saddened by the hatred shown toward homosexuals in the name of Jesus Christ. The oft-quoted Biblical verse used to justify this most un-Christian attitude is Leviticus 18:22, which states, "Do not lie with a man as one lies with a woman; that is detestable."

Despite my intense fear of the Old Testament, I read through Leviticus and discovered that, in addition to homosexuality, the Old Testament condemns a lot of other actions over which most Christians don't lose sleep. For example, Leviticus is very clear about the practice of eating shellfish: "Anything living in the water that does not have fins and scales is to be detestable to you" (Lev. 11:12). Despite the fact that the word *detestable* is used, I've yet to hear a preacher rant about the evils of shrimp cocktail. Pigs aren't viewed favorably in the Bible either. Leviticus 11:7-8 reminds us that they are unclean animals whose meat should not be eaten, and whose carcasses should not be touched. Why, then, aren't Christians boycotting McDonald's restaurants that sell the popular McRib sandwich? And let's not forget what Leviticus says about polyester: "Do not wear clothing woven of two kinds of materials" (Lev. 19:19). Ladies and gentlemen, I hate to break it to you, but it looks like the entire original cast of *The Brady Bunch* is going to Hell.

As I write this, the Episcopal Church is recovering from a painful, public struggle involving the appointment of Gene Robinson as the denomination's first openly gay bishop. I applaud the church leaders' efforts to create an environment that is truly welcoming to all of God's children, and I thank the Lord every day that I found a parish that is open-minded, tolerant, and radically compassionate. I can only hope that, in the midst of this conflict, Episcopalians will reread Luke before storming off in a huff and advocating schism. I also hope that they can shed some light upon the Old Testament's condemnation of polyester.

My friend Angela says that some straight Christians enjoy condemning gays because homosexuality is the one "sin" they can feel confident about never committing. We've all coveted our neighbors' goods and talked trash about our mother and fathers. As far as the sin of adultery goes, more people probably *would* commit adultery if anyone besides their spouse found them remotely attractive. And while most of us will never kill another human being, we're guilty of supporting murderous political regimes by buying cheap clothing and other materials from third-world countries that violate human rights and child labor laws. So how does one feel superior in these murky waters we call life? How does one assuage his or her guilt about committing so many "little" sins every day? By making homosexuality a "big" sin.

If Jesus returns to this earth anytime soon, I'm sure that he'll recruit a couple of drag queens for his entourage, just to annoy the televangelists. After all, in this day and age, tax collectors and hemorrhaging women don't raise the ire of average Americans like a 300-pound guy in cha-cha heels can.

———— ⬤ ————

Maybe it's the manager in me, but, in the midst of the Bible study, I decided to examine my own personal take on the Bible and define a core set of beliefs regarding its relevance and application in my life. For those of you keeping score at home, I have come to believe that the Bible is a divinely inspired text. I do not think, however, that God spoke directly to its authors, who then transcribed the words, verbatim, onto parchment like manic administrative assistants. Rather, I believe that God's Spirit guided the hearts and minds of the individuals who wrote the text of the Christian Bible, and that he allowed for a little poetic license to give the narrative a better flow.

I believe that the Bible came together to help a nascent and disparate Christian community unite under a banner of similar ideas and consistent theological tenets, thus creating common ground and establishing some authority. In order to qualify as a true religion, creeds and accepted beliefs need to be established. This is no different from a business or non-profit organization creating a mission statement, or a political party adopting a platform. Without a common set of beliefs, a sense of community and a sense of purpose will never emerge.

When John wrote his Gospel seventy years after Jesus' crucifixion, he was trying to appeal to a young church that was no longer predominantly Jewish. It was also a time in which some Christians were placing undue emphasis on John the Baptist, while others were arguing that God did not create the heavens and earth. William Barclay tells us that "the aim of the writer of the Fourth Gospel was to present the Christian faith in such a way that it would commend itself to the Greek world to which Christianity had gone out, and also to combat the heresies and mistaken ideas which had arisen within the Church."

Yes, John had an agenda.

The fact that I choose not to read the Bible "literally" does not mean that I cannot view it as a holy text that is both meaningful to my life and crucial to the existence and promulgation of Christianity as a whole. For example, I believe that God inspired Luke to record his understanding of Jesus' teachings, and that God's fingerprints are all over it. But I've also come to believe that Luke was a poet and dreamer who liked to embellish a bit for the sake of a good story. Did Mary really burst out into the gorgeous Magnificat, as recorded in Luke 1:46, exclaiming, "My soul magnifies the Lord, and my spirit has rejoiced in God my Savior"? Probably not. But the words attributed to her are beautiful and meaningful nonetheless, and they have comforted Christians in their faith journeys for centuries.

I also believe that Handel's *Messiah,* Beethoven's *Ninth Symphony,* and everything Stevie Wonder released between 1972 and 1976 were divinely inspired as well. Does this mean that God held the hands of George Friederic, Ludwig, and Stevie as they tickled the ivories and wrote some of the most transcendent melodies ever to spill out into the universe? No. But the music of great artists comes from a place that few of us writers and musicians will ever visit. And so it is with the words of the Bible.

So why is it that some Christians want their Bible verses fed to them in big, literal spoonfuls? For the same reason that artists like Jessica Simpson and Michael Bolton have sold millions of albums. Stay with me for a moment. See, most Americans are content to limit their musical horizons to the pabulum that pours out of corporate-owned, mainstream radio stations. Listeners are told that the songs being played are "good," and, as a result, they begin to believe that they are. If consumers were to stop accepting this supposed truth, then they would be forced to explore other types of music via the Internet or the alternative press. Then they would discover bands whose CDs cannot be found at the local Kmart or Target store.

Because the CDs that the newly emancipated listener learns about can't be found at Kmart, he or she will have to drive two towns over to shop at the cool, independent record store near the college. Once exposed to interesting music, he or she will no longer tolerate the inane drivel played on MTV or Top 40 radio stations, which means that the listener will have to buy a CD player for his or her car. And so on.

See, it's a whole lot easier to just nod your head in agreement when the DJ starts talking about how brilliant Britney Spears's newest single is. Disagreeing with the DJ means that there is work to be done, and we as a nation are huge fans of the path of least resistance; hence, Michael Bolton's platinum record sales.

By the same token, it is easier to be told exactly what to think about Christianity than to allow for the messiness of contextual truths and mystery to add some gray to the black-and-white mix. This is not to say that non-literal denominations "make it up as they go along," or that they waiver in the belief that Jesus Christ is the Son of God. No, those of us who don't interpret the Bible literally simply feel that it's possible to revel in the rich symbolism and colorful details surrounding a story such as that of Jonah and the whale without insisting that Jonah actually lived inside a giant fish for three days before being vomited onto dry land.

Can God really be contained between the embossed leather covers of a book? Did God really stop revealing himself after Chapter 22 of the Book of Revelation? Does God really want the goal of our spiritual life to be "comfort," the kind of comfort derived from feeling certain and superior? We don't go to the gym to be comfortable; rather, we go there to sweat, to strain, and ultimately, to be transformed. Likewise, rather than expecting Christianity to answer every single one of our questions, shouldn't we be willing to let Christianity question some of our answers?

Either way, I'm pretty sure that polyester *is* evil on some level.

12
Five O'Clock World

Some of the best religious discussions in which I engaged during my early days as a Christian took place at the public library. I find this a bit ironic, as public institution administrators get nervous when employees so much as utter the word *Jesus*. And they should get nervous because, after all, the public library is *public*, and the public is composed of everyone from atheists to Buddhists to folks who believe that aliens are coming to whisk us away. So these conversations took place behind closed doors.

According to author Robert Hughes, public libraries are also "veritable lighthouses of Utopian order and generosity amid the clutter and ignorance and selfishness of so much of the life that is lived in this world." I've taped this passage on my computer so that I can reread it on particularly difficult workdays.

But I digress . . .

While collaborating on a system-wide library project, I informed an associate named Julia that I'd joined an Episcopalian church. In turn, Julia told me that she was a "cradle Episcopalian" who hadn't set foot in a church since both of her parents died some years before. She proceeded to ask me some questions, and we engaged in a long discussion about faith. Next thing I knew, she not only joined St.

Andrew's, but signed up to make some noise in the church's hand bell choir.

Let it be known that, had Julia not shown any interest in my newfound identity, I would have changed the subject immediately. I don't believe in cramming God down the throats of those who don't share my enthusiasm. Nor would I ever use my status as a manager to intimidate a subordinate into listening to a spiel about the Episcopal Church. Such an action would not only be illegal, it would be downright tacky. Becoming a shining light for Christ does *not* entitle me to blind the person standing in front of me.

However, when an administrator told me that I couldn't conduct a "Secret Santa" gift exchange at my library location for fear of offending non-Christians, I felt as though he were taking that whole "separation of church and state" ruling a bit too far; after all, I don't remember reading anything in the Gospels about eight tiny reindeer and a fat guy in a red suit visiting the Christ child. Regardless, in an effort to respect the religious diversity of everyone involved, my co-workers and I changed the phrase "Secret Santa" to "Secret Generic Holiday Friend." So far, we haven't offended anybody.

Jared, a twenty-something library assistant, mentioned his enthusiasm for the writings of C. S. Lewis one day. I informed him that I'd just finished reading a biography of Lewis, and before I knew it we were caught up in a heavy theological discussion in my office. Upon learning of the seventeen years I spent adrift in a dark swamp of atheism, Jared lamented, "I've never lost my faith. I mean, if for one second I thought that God did not exist, I'd throw in the towel. But the fact that I've never questioned or doubted God's existence makes me feel . . . shallow. . . ."

How do you respond to a comment like that?

"Consider yourself lucky," I offered. "You've always had God along for the ride."

"But God gave us rational thought," he continued, "and he gave us the ability to question his existence, something I've never done. What's wrong with me?"

I felt sorry for Jared. Let's face it, "awakening" stories are much more interesting than those of faithful Christians who keep showing up to church week after week. This is why I never made it through Thérèse of Lisieux's spiritual classic *Story of a Soul.* After plowing through ninety pages of the author's unwavering faith, good works, and disciplined prayer life, I exclaimed, "When does she get drunk and lose her virginity in the back seat of a Chevy?" before tossing the book across the room in disgust. I crave dramatic tension and transformation in my spiritual literature.

If prolific Christian author Philip Yancey had been in on the conversation, he probably would've brought up the concept of "faith personalities." Since some of us possess pensive, melancholy demeanors, while others are annoyingly happy-go-lucky, it only makes sense that our understanding and expression of faith, or "faith personalities," will be just as diverse. There will always be those folks who must drift, wrestle, and doubt, just as we will always have Christians who are steadfast in their convictions. There is no "correct" method for experiencing God.

While my co-worker was coveting my prodigal son experience, I found myself envying his tale of blessed assurance. How much easier life would've been if I'd never turned my back on God. Think of all the wonderful people I would have met and the profound books I could've read. Perhaps, instead of library school, I might have ended up at seminary, where I'd have learned to counsel other drifters and doubters.

Oh, but what's the point of speculating? Regardless of my bad choices and aimless amblings, I was right where I needed to be. Despite the odds, I'd embraced God, found a loving congregation, and, perhaps most important, been transformed by the pain I'd experienced on my way there. Had my path been all roses and scenic summits, then maybe the passion I felt for God would have waned by this point. Maybe I needed the trial by fire to get here, and maybe, just maybe, my stubborn, defiant faith personality was a blessing rather than a curse.

"It's all good, Jared."

What else could I say?

@ @ @

While straightening the shelves and tidying up the periodicals room, I almost always encounter religious pamphlets tucked into books or propped up for everyone to see. Because I believe in the sanctity of the public library, I toss them in the recycling bin, just as I toss the political party pamphlets and "hot, horny co-eds online" postcards that also appear unbidden. But I have to wonder: has anyone ever come to know God through those little inspirational tracts that litter the landscape? And what about those "Jesus Saves" billboards? Has anyone had a spiritual awakening right out on the main thoroughfare because of some clever slogan pasted up in big letters by the town's wealthier congregations?

For those of us who don't have access to a pulpit or a printing press, perhaps the best way to spread God's message of love and redemption is to simply walk the walk, much as Brenda did when we worked together in Alamance County. I never said "I want what she has" because of the things she said, but because of the things she did. She was kind to people. She was patient. She treated everyone she encountered with the respect and dignity owed a child of God.

The fact that she did this on a consistent basis is impressive, because working with the public is not easy. When that rude lady with the feathered 1980s hairdo shouts at me because she can't find a copy of Danielle Steel's latest literary masterpiece on the shelf, I remind myself that she's one of God's children. Sometimes God's kids call you nasty names and refuse to get off the computer at closing time. On occasion, they'll be drunk and have to be escorted out of the library by a policeman. But God loves them all, even when I can't. God feels their pain when I'm too exhausted or personally offended to care anymore. And God is always waiting for them with open arms when I just wish they'd go away.

As I walked out to my mailbox one afternoon, I spotted a clunky moving van parked in front of Tammy's house. I hadn't thought about her much in recent weeks, as her gang of wayward adolescents had moved on to to greener pastures since I'd taken God's advice and talked to them. Maybe, in addition to the attention of the knucklehead across the street, Tammy had also wanted to get *my* attention. Perhaps the simple act of acknowledging her existence was all it took for her to stop making noise and trying to get noticed.

I wandered around the cul-de-sac, but Tammy was nowhere to be found. It occurred to me that I'd never gotten a chance to ask her about herself. Did she like school? What sort of music did she listen to? Was she happy? What did she fantasize about becoming when she got older? What saddened me most of all was the fact that I didn't get to thank her for bringing me to my knees and invoking the name of God. For whatever reason, God chose to use Tammy as a conduit for my own personal kaboom, even though she had no idea that she was even listed on that evening's program.

Sure, my spiritual awakening story would have been more dramatic had I heard the voice of God while trapped in a burning building or while squirreled away in the trunk of a kidnapper's vehicle. Burning bushes and plagues make for pretty good headlines as well. Instead, I owe it all to a noisy teenager whose little sister rang my doorbell and ran a few times.

"So, Karen," you might have thought a few chapters back, "you're telling me that you fell to your knees because some kids were singing pop songs in front of your house? Isn't that kind of lame?"

Yes, it's very lame, and even more ridiculous. Yet, it worked. Who am I to argue with God's methods?

Tammy, if you don't currently have the gift of faith, may you someday find it. May you avoid the usual pitfalls along the way. May you open your heart and mind to the possibility of a loving God who works to transform us in our pain. And may you find peace, wherever you are.

13

Sins of Omission

On the day that I was confirmed

as an Episcopalian, my parents did not make me feel bad for abandoning the faith of my childhood. No, the simple fact that their younger daughter had chosen to join a Christian denomination that did not involve snake handling or cyanide-laced Kool-Aid was more than enough to make them happy. I, however, felt the crushing guilt involved in abandoning the "One True Church" for at least the first couple of months at St. Andy's. Having to drive past Our Lady of Grace Catholic Church on my way there every Sunday only compounded this temporary spate of hard-earned Catholic neurosis.

Shortly after confirmation, some acquaintances and I took a trip to Ocracoke Island, on the Outer Banks of North Carolina. The laid-back fishing village is chock full of seafood restaurants, funky gift shops, and quaint bookstores, each one featuring a fat, lazy cat to greet you on the steps. There are no golden arches or shopping malls on the island, making it a veritable Garden of Eden in my book.

As I fondled an overpriced, faux-stained-glass bookmark in an artsy bookshop, it occurred to me that I hadn't spotted a single Christian title in the whole place. I had no trouble locating a collection of poems by the Sufi poet Rumi, two books by the Dalai Lama, and something by Oonagh Shanley-Toffolo, the late Princess Di's psychic advisor, but nothing with "Jesus" as a subject heading.

Perhaps the proprietor has the luxury of stocking only books that she personally fancies, or found Christian literature to be a tough sell out on the island. But in my mind, the message flashed loud and clear: Christianity is *not* compatible with "artsy" or "funky." People who appreciate groovy, overpriced earrings and unusual pottery are probably too cool to adhere to the tenets of a religion as un-hip as Christianity.

Okay, maybe I was being a bit hypersensitive because I was still so new to the whole Jesus thing. But as I got back to Greensboro, I couldn't help but notice that, while the organic food co-op I patronize stocks plenty of Hindu and Buddhist doo-dads, one would be at a loss to locate a single Christian item. And whenever Jesus or Mary pop up in the artwork displayed at either of my two favorite coffee houses, it's solely for "kitsch" or "camp" value.

It's ironic that the artsy, counterculture crowd is so quick to turn its back on Jesus when the Son of God was a pretty countercultural guy. Aside from African-American R&B singers, when was the last time you heard a white actor or rock 'n' roll musician (besides Mel Gibson and those guys in Creed) talk in great detail about going to church, praying, or reading the Bible? In a recent *National Enquirer* article about the spiritual life of the stars, I came across many references to the Kabbalah, meditation, Scientology, and Buddhism, but the closest that anyone came to discussing Christianity involved a flaky discussion about angels.

When I mentioned this observation to a non-Christian friend, her response was sarcastic.

"Oh, you poor, oppressed Christian. It's bad enough that it says 'In God We Trust' on our money, but now you're bitching because you can't find a copy of the New Testament in your favorite health food store!"

I need to make some new friends.

I informed her that I was not suggesting that Christians in America are oppressed. Rather, my consternation involved the fact that, thanks to the negative images that many people have of Christianity and Christians, countless numbers of educated, cutting-edge artist-types will never embrace Jesus when they are empty, hurting, and desperate. Maybe they'll try to convince themselves that they'd be happy if they only became more successful or found the right lover. They'll chase the latest spiritual trend or seek out non-stop distractions so that they can avoid what their cool peers consider to be an archaic, outdated, and utterly irrelevant faith.

Oprah regular Deepak Chopra and his ilk don't help matters any when they denounce religion as antithetical to enlightenment. "I personally feel that all organized religion takes you away from spirituality," he had the audacity to declare. "This is true of Hinduism and Buddhism as well. Spirituality is supposed to free you. To give you the experience of unbounded freedom. All organized religions do exactly the opposite. They're judgmental. They impose punishment. Every religion is fear-based."

Sorry, Deepak, but I've yet to be sent to bed with no Communion wafers for screwing up the Nicene Creed during worship service.

And then there's my favorite television show, the one whose scripts I've practically memorized, the show from which I've collected everything from lunchboxes to automobile air fresheners. Yes, I'm talking about *The Simpsons,* the sweetest slice of satire ever to grace the small screen. The show's most visible Christian is Ned Flanders, Homer's remarkably dorky, God-fearing neighbor. His kids are mini-dorks, and his wife is a snooty hypocrite whose sole motivation for attending Bible camp was "learning how to be more judgmental." Reverend Lovejoy, Ned's unenthusiastic minister, once advised the annoying character to join another religion, since they're all "basically the same." And in one Halloween episode, Ned Flanders turned out to be Satan himself.

Yeah, I know, it probably sounds like I'm revisiting the "Dan Quayle vs. Murphy Brown" debate. I should also mention that policemen, elementary school teachers, and bar owners in the animated fictional town of Springfield don't come off looking too good either. But at least we can find positive portrayals of cops, teachers, and purveyors of pilsner on *other* television shows.

It seems like the only time we're likely to encounter positive portrayals of church attendance is in those movies or TV shows about fun, effusive ethnic families. Greeks talk about church in *My Big Fat Greek Wedding.* Italians go to church in Mafioso flicks. Sometimes Irish Catholics go to church when they're not busy suffering through potato famines or getting rip-roaring drunk. As long as worship is referenced in the context of ethnic identity, then the audience doesn't get too nervous.

When WASPy Protestants go to church, however, the experience is usually portrayed in a negative light. The Baptist minister in *Footloose* tried to break Kevin Bacon's spirit by declaring that dancing was the handiwork of the devil. *Carrie*'s Jesus-freak mom stuck her in the closet whenever the teen expressed an interest in the opposite sex or the latest fashions. The creepy Christian lady that played hymns on her Casio keyboard in *Edward Scissorhands* announced to the neighbors that the sweet, misunderstood protagonist was the devil. And in *The People vs. Larry Flynt,* Jerry Falwell, the Christian that everyone loves to hate, tried to rain on the lovable Larry's porn parade and quash his attempts at exercising his First Amendment rights.

I recently saw two movies that followed this trend. *The Good Girl,* an interesting little independent film starring Jennifer Aniston, features a Christian character played by Michael White. As the movie progresses, we discover that this cheerful Retail Rodeo security guard is actually a perverted voyeur who watches Jennifer and her much younger co-worker fool around in the storage room. On the night that I saw the movie, the audience erupted in laughter after White's character gets beaten up due to a misunderstanding with Jennifer's husband; the damn Christian got what he deserved.

Igby Goes Down, one of the more pointless and unlikable movies I've seen, features a rich, messed-up, but very smart high school kid who has been kicked out of every expensive prep school on the East Coast. In one scene, Igby is waxing philosophical with a priest when he makes the following statement, which I will paraphrase, because I would have no choice but to sit through the movie again to quote it exactly: "If Heaven is so f%$#&n great, then why was the crucifixion supposedly so hard?" Instead of responding, the priest just sits and stares in silence. Igby grins. The audience grins. The hero has beaten the stuffy old priest at his own game.

If I'd seen this flick prior to my awakening, I wouldn't have even blinked an eye. Seeing it as a Christian, however, made me furious. No man or woman of the cloth would sit idly in response to such a question. Why was the crucifixion so hard? Because Jesus was fully human when he came to join us on earth. He felt physical and mental pain, just like any of us. Despite the promise of God's kingdom, Jesus knew that someone would be pounding nails through his flesh in the very near future. This is why the crucifixion was so hard and such a big deal.

OK, Igby?

I'm not implying that a vast anti-Christian media conspiracy exists. I do not believe that those who create and sell funky art and tofu products secretly hate Christians, or that they place subliminal messages in their overpriced knickknacks and vegetarian fare. What I'm struggling with is the lack of positive Christian role models in popular music, primetime television, and the arts, and how it can greatly affect individuals like myself who might otherwise have turned to God earlier in their lives.

Even though my high school friends and I were involved in a Catholic youth group, we constantly teased a classmate of ours who was just a bit too sincere about her faith. Lisa never preached, and she didn't act holier than thou. No, we targeted her because she had the nerve to listen to Amy Grant records and attend Catholic youth retreats on the weekends. Very un-cool.

The members of Generation X, as well as our younger peers in Generation "whatever they're calling it these days," are a cynical lot. We are not easily impressed. We roll our eyes a lot, and enjoy hosting campy Brady Bunch trivia contests and disco parties. Genuine displays of emotion are looked down upon, and sincerity is flat-out embarrassing. No wonder the Christian faith seems so foreign to those of us who are overly concerned with being ironic, sarcastic, and campy.

Becoming a Christian requires a bit of risk taking. When we dare to humble ourselves before God by getting on our knees, when we stand naked before him, warts and all, we relinquish power and control. When we embrace Jesus Christ, we are admitting that we don't have all of the answers. When we ask for forgiveness for our sins, we are forced to take ownership of the unkind things we have done to our neighbors. And when we are willing to succumb to the beauty of something that cannot be "proven" by a mathematical equation or a panel of experts, we have to rely on faith and faith alone. So why do we do it? Because it's worth the risk.

Of course, falling in love requires just as many risks, but that hasn't stopped most of the world from jumping head first into one rocky relationship after another. Yes, when we open our hearts to another, we relinquish control. Very often, we suffer disappointment when the object of our affection turns out to be a little less perfect than we'd once believed. And, as we've all found out, healthy relationships require work and eternal vigilance. But we do it anyway. Why? Because it's worth the risk. Or, as Woody Allen so eloquently stated in *Annie Hall,* "Because we need the eggs."

The more time I spend attending services at St. Andrew's, reading books about the Christian faith, and fumbling through my prayer life, the more "liberal" my outlook on life has become. This may come as a surprise to those who equate being religious with being right-wing, or who view altruistic acts done in the name of God as somehow suspect. But once I became determined to try to view *all* people as children of God, it became more and more difficult to dismiss, ignore, or hate anyone.

Not that I was running around kicking old ladies and stealing candy from babies before becoming a Christian, mind you. Rather, I was a bit like the folks in the parable of the Good Samaritan who ignored the bleeding man on the side of the road; they weren't in the wrong for having *done* something bad, but for having *neglected to do* something good. Of course, advocating the stance that we try to view all persons as deserving of love and respect is no less radical today than it was in Jesus' time.

We live in a globally powerful nation that views the men, women, and children in third world countries as nothing more than pawns to be exploited for the benefit of those in the West. When our nation's leaders support crooked dictators because they are friendly to U.S. economic interests, they are not viewing all people as the children of God. When a country spends one million dollars a year to maintain an aircraft carrier when the same amount of money could be used to build 17,000 homes for 67,000 people, enroll 384,000 more kids in Head Start, or give 500,000 children in the U.S. three meals a day for a year, the children of God are not priority number one.

As I watched the horrific footage of Iraqi prisoners being abused at Abu Ghraib, I was dismayed and disgusted. Yet, I can't say that I was especially shocked. In the months leading up to the war, we were told that Iraqis are somehow "less than" Americans. If they weren't, then how could we collectively justify a bombing campaign in which innocent civilians were murdered? How can we expect a bunch of scared blue-collar military kids who have been indoctrinated to believe that Arabs are uncivilized, freedom-hating heathens to then treat these same Arabs with dignity and respect? When we are selective about whom we view as God's children, then why are we surprised when certain individuals are treated as anything but?

In an effort to channel my despair, I argue with warmongers and write op-ed pieces defending the Dixie Chicks' right to free speech. I put clever bumper stickers on my car that say things like "Draft SUV Drivers First." I remind people that God does not cause violence and suffering; rather, he put the world in our hands, and we've made it what it is today.

I've gotten pretty good at standing up for the oppressed masses on paper and in verbal confrontations, but I could still use some work on interacting with God's children one-on-one. For example, while I was rushing out of the library one day to run a personal errand, a wide-eyed woman asked me if the restroom had a sanitary pad dispenser.

"No, sorry," I replied as I made a beeline toward my fuel-efficient car.

I pulled onto the street and immediately chastised myself for not having taken two minutes to walk back into my office with the woman to retrieve a pad from my emergency stash. Why had I been so quick to say "No," avoid eye contact, and go on my merry way? Because I've spent an entire lifetime perfecting my "go away" stare and honing my ability to look right through people. It was a knee-jerk reaction, one that I will need to spend a great deal of energy dismantling if I truly want to walk with Jesus.

Yes, we live in a dangerous world, and I would not advocate picking up hitchhikers, taking a violent crack addict into your home to "dry out," or giving your life savings away to every panhandler in Manhattan in the misguided belief that doing so will somehow end hunger. Nor will performing random acts of kindness bring an end to war or redistribute wealth. But if we begin slowing down and choosing to acknowledge the people with whom we coexist, then doing so will eventually become a habit. If we take the time to listen and reach out more than we do, then, instead of avoiding eye contact with the woman in search of a maxipad, our knee-jerk reaction will be to say "Oh, man, I've been there myself. Come to my office for a second."

Barbara Taylor Brown captures the phenomenon of interpersonal alienation perfectly in a collection of sermons titled *Gospel Medicine.* She decided to start using public transportation because of a commitment to the environment, but hadn't considered the social consequences of doing so. While on a Greyhound bus bound for Augusta, Georgia, she clamped her Walkman on tightly and pulled out her theology journals while life pulsated and breathed all around her. She writes:

> Once we got underway, it was like a block party on wheels. People asked each other their names and tried to figure out if they knew any of the same people in Augusta. They passed fried chicken around and fell asleep on each other's shoulders. They held each other's screaming babies and traded stories that made them howl with laughter, while the middle-class white lady, sitting

up front all by herself, turned up the volume on her Walkman and read about the kingdom of God.

Of course, having seen *Planes, Trains and Automobiles* one too many times on Comedy Central, I can totally relate to the desire to turn up the volume and avoid potentially annoying passengers. Besides, I am not a bubbly, outgoing person by nature. So is there a "right" answer to this scenario? No. Do I have any easy answers? No again. All I know is that, since my conversion I've worked hard at trying to smile more at the public service desk. I've made peace with the fact that children cry and talk loudly, and I don't get stressed about it at work or at restaurants like I used to. And I've made more of an effort to engage people in conversation, even when I don't have to. As a result, work has been a heck of a lot more pleasant.

If my Christian conversion led me away from the likes of Marilyn Manson and Eminem, it led me straight toward the late, great Johnny Cash. I'd always been a fan of songs like "Folsom Prison Blues" and "A Boy Named Sue," but, until I read the Man in Black's autobiography, I had no idea what a great Christian role model he really is.

To many folks, Johnny was just a gruff country singer who battled drug addiction and recorded some memorable tunes. Upon contemplating his life and music more deeply, however, I began viewing him as nothing short of a messenger. He sang to everyone from presidents to prisoners because, in Johnny's eyes, we're all children of God. He wore black not as a fashion statement, but to show solidarity with the poor, the hungry, and the hopeless. He took us to task for dismissing "the lonely voice of youth," and put together a whole album's worth of songs about the plight of the American Indian long before it was politically correct to do such a thing. And when he walked away from Sun Records, it wasn't because of money, but the simple fact that Sam Phillips wouldn't let him record a gospel album.

Like a colorful character from the Old Testament, Johnny Cash found God after crawling into a cave. The amphetamine-addled star could no longer tolerate the massive chasm that existed between himself and God, and lay down to die alone in the darkness. Then he became conscious of the fact that he was not in charge of his destiny, and opened his heart to Jesus on the spot. He would continue to struggle with addiction in the years to come, but he never lost his faith in the God that pulled him out of the cave that day, the God who kept forgiving and loving him when others had all but given up.

Despite his compassion and charity, Johnny was remarkably humble. He writes:

> I don't have Paul's calling—I'm not out there being all things to all men to win them for Christ—but sometimes I can be a signpost. Sometimes I can sow a seed. And post-hole diggers and seed sowers are mighty important in the building of the Kingdom.

That's all that most of us can do.

Let's face it, Cash is no C. S. Lewis. But when I'm traveling down that long stretch of lonesome, a place where hope and joy can't be found for miles, I glean more comfort from the honest, simple songs of Johnny Cash than from the eloquent prose of *Mere Christianity.*

Thank God for the messengers. And thank God for the fact that all of his messengers are *not* created in the image of Ned Flanders or Jerry Falwell!

14

"Talk to Them"

One year had passed since I'd embraced God on that warm winter afternoon, one year since my entire world was rocked, slammed, and turned inside out. And what did I have to show for it? A loving second family, peace of mind, and a sense of direction and purpose. Not bad for a year's work, eh? Of course, these things were not handed to me in a silver chalice. I had to want them and then work for them, as nothing worthwhile in life comes easy. Let's face it, if people really could develop washboard abs in eight minutes a day or master the guitar in a week, then Brad Pitt and Eric Clapton would both be looking for new jobs.

Had I not plugged in to a congregation, I am convinced that my interest in Christianity, like Buddhism before it, would have devolved from a spiritual pursuit to merely an intellectual one. Believing in God is not enough unto itself, as any belief can be swayed when a better argument or more attractive option emerges. No, it was crucial that I had an opportunity to *experience* God on a regular basis, not through burning bushes, kabooms, or claps of thunder, but through the work that his followers do. I needed to see God's love in action on a regular basis.

So I go to church. I show up on those days when I'm feeling insecure and small and can barely squeak out the Lord's Prayer. Sometimes I hear a sermon that strikes a chord so rich and powerful that it reverberates for weeks, while other sermons drift by like so much background music. There are Sunday mornings when my soul does cartwheels and threatens to spill all over the pew, and others in which I can barely keep my eyes open.

So I go to church. It is here that I take part in familiar rituals that draw God down from his lofty throne and make him tangible and close at hand. It is here that I can both drink from and contribute to the strength and faith of the congregation. It is here that I can slow down and be fully present, praising God for his patience and love while renewing the wonderful gift of faith that was bestowed upon me.

Back in my atheist wasteland days, I posed the incendiary question "Is God so insecure that he needs us to praise him?" to a religious acquaintance of mine. I can't remember how she responded, but I do know how I would respond here and now: No, God doesn't *need* our praise and worship; it's just that we can't help ourselves.

@　@　@

In that first year as a Christian, I found myself unrelentingly drawn to books about spirituality. Sure, I still managed to squeeze a trashy rock star biography in now and then, but my desire to know God and understand the basic tenets of my faith was overwhelming. "So many books, so little time," is a phrase I still hear myself muttering as I look over the latest offering of religious titles to roll off the presses.

One such book that has become a favorite of mine is *Reluctant Saint,* Donald Spoto's colorful biography of St. Francis of Assisi. In a nutshell, pre-conversion Francis was a hedonistic thirteenth-century party boy who loved to sing in public and fantasize about fame. Needless to say, I could identify with him. And then one day, in order to escape the heat and humidity, a weary and disillusioned Francis ducked into a neglected, decrepit church. He sat down, chilled out, and stared at the simple crucifix stretched over the altar. From out of the blue, the crucifix spoke to him, saying: "Francis, don't you see that my house is being destroyed? Go then, and rebuild it for me."

Party-boy Francis was hardly what the townsfolk would call deserving of a divine message. He had come to church not to seek God, but to escape the humidity. Yet, God chose him as the recipient of a very important charge. And because Francis had no reference point for what was happening, he fixed up the abandoned church in which he was sitting. Of course, we all know that the beloved saint would go on to rebuild the Church with a capital *C*, but who could really blame him for initially picking up a hammer and getting to work on foundations and window frames?

"How cute," I thought upon reading the passage, "he interpreted God's words literally."

It was then that I experienced an epiphany of sorts. Hadn't I also taken God's message literally? When God suggested that I "talk to them" on that blessed afternoon, I'd assumed that he was referring to the tangible objects of my derision, and I didn't bother to deconstruct the message. I'd simply talked to *them*, the teenagers standing right outside my house.

Based on the Francis example, couldn't "them" refer to more than that which was immediately within reach? And couldn't "talk" also mean "write" or "sing"? In the same way that God wanted Francis to rebuild the Church with a capital *C*, does God want me to talk to Them with a capital *T*? Don't worry, I am not comparing my own inadequate religious path to that of one of the greatest men to ever call himself a Christian, but Francis's conversion story does make me wonder just what God has in store for me.

I suppose that writing this book is one way I've chosen to "talk to them," whoever and wherever they may be. The two secular novels I wrote in my twenties never did find a publisher; maybe they were just practice books, a means of sharpening my writing skills so that, when I finally had something relevant to say, I'd have a way to say it.

I've also chosen to "talk to them" by ditching the puerile rock star fantasies and forming a gospel trio with two friends from the church choir. Our ever-growing repertoire includes such classic hymns as "I'll Fly Away" and "Shall We Gather at the River," golden oldies that were completely new to this former atheist. Soon our as-yet-unnamed trio will be visiting nursing homes and homeless shelters, spreading God's message of love and forgiveness via three-part harmony. No, I haven't tossed out my rock 'n' roll CDs or stopped singing Beatles songs in the shower, but the joy I feel after playing songs of praise is greater than any I'd felt after performing with Shannon or my old pals from the Seven Oasis.

Of course, insecure gal that I am, there are days on which I'm convinced that God would never choose to work through a tremendously flawed person with a checkered past like myself. I have no problem accepting the fact that God likes to work through broken people when I read about *other* Christians, but I wrestle with the validity of my own experience. St. Francis was hardly a pillar of the community, and, as Donald Spoto so eloquently elucidates, he may have not been the most mentally stable person to have ever preached Christ's message either:

> It has to be acknowledged that Francis was also an eccentric, as saints tend to be. As much as we might prefer them to be polite traditional-ists who never upset our certainties or challenge our mediocrities, they are resoundingly not normal people, for how indeed does one remain somnolently normal after being shaken to the roots by an encounter with God, however imperfectly perceived?

Would St. Francis have passed the psychological exams currently required for Episcopal seminary aspirants? I doubt it. But he still managed to "rebuild" the church, and, despite the odds, enticed believers back to Jesus' message of radical compassion during a time in which the Church was more interested in money and power than in fixing broken people.

I hurriedly prepared for church, yanking on a pair of pantyhose that had about three good hours left in them while thinking about Bob, St. Andrew's esteemed elderly librarian. He had just suffered a stroke, and the prospect of returning to life as he knew it did not look promising. We'd engaged in weekly chats about politics, theology, and favorite books, and I was determined to continue our regular chats, no matter where they'd end up taking place.

I dealt with my despair by creating an oversized "Get Well" card featuring a caricature of my friend reading a big, fat theology book; the caption below said, "Bob relaxes with a little light beach reading." I stopped by Krispy Kreme on the way to St. Andy's to stock up on crullers and custard-filled donuts so that, after the service, everyone could come to the library for a card-signing celebration.

As I stood in line decked out in my skirt and favorite sweater, it occurred to me that the men and women sipping coffee and reading the *Greensboro News & Record* in their sweat pants and baseball caps could probably deduce that I was on my way to church; as a result, I felt oddly special. Not superior or judgmental, mind you, but special, because I was part of the massive Christian throng that gets up early on Sunday mornings to praise our Creator in the company of our peers. As I stood in line for my donuts, I felt overwhelmingly connected to the big, fat, dysfunctional Christian family, a family composed of Catholics and Protestants, sinners and saints, the crazy guy with the giant cross who shouted Scripture passages outside of the Student Union building at UMass and those who quietly acted on their faith. I was kin to those Christians who snuck into the last pew and those who preached from the pulpit, Democrats and Republicans, homosexuals and heterosexuals, African-American women in wildly creative hats boasting feathers and fruit as well as proper Episcopalian ladies in white gloves and pearls. For one fleeting moment, I felt part of something bigger than myself, something that lives and breathes and keeps on growing.

Yes, we are all connected, not by our own unique rituals and prejudices, but by our mutual desire to strengthen our relationship with God. We fight, we point fingers, and we segregate ourselves from one another, but we're all in the same boat, all searching for Jesus, some convinced they have found him, some purporting to speak for him, and some convinced that they'll never even get close.

We are family, every last one of us, each with our scars and each in his or her own ridiculous packaging. We stumble, dust ourselves off, and keep on searching for wisdom. Sometimes it comes on the wings of a prophet or in the words of a learned theologian, and sometimes our eyes are opened because of noisy teenagers, country music, and donuts.

And I wouldn't want it any other way.

Notes

INTRODUCTION

Taylor, Barbara Brown. *Gospel Medicine* (Boston, MA: Cowley Publications, 1995), 159.

CHAPTER TWO

Aucoin, Don. "State's French Hide Strength in Numbers," *Boston Globe* (September 21, 1997), B1, B4.

Morrissey, Bill. *Edson* (New York, NY: Alfred A. Knopf, 1996), 4.

Hampl, Patricia. *Virgin Time* (New York, NY: Ballantine Books, 1992), 67.

CHAPTER THREE

Lee, Tommy, et al. *Mötley Crüe: The Dirt* (New York, NY: Regan Books, 2001), 217.

Rand, Ayn. *The Fountainhead* (New York, NY: Signet, 1993), 686.

CHAPTER FIVE

Lamott, Anne. *Traveling Mercies: Some Thoughts on Faith* (New York, NY: Pantheon Books, 1999), 49.

CHAPTER SIX

Bonaduce, Danny. *Random Acts of Badness* (New York, NY: Hyperion, 2001), 269.

CHAPTER EIGHT

Malone, Nancy M. *Walking A Literary Labyrinth: A Spirituality of Reading* (New York, NY: Riverhead Books, 2003), 32.

McLennan, Scotty. *Finding Your Religion: When the Faith You Grew up with Has Lost Its Meaning* (San Francisco, CA: Harper, 1999), 13.

CHAPTER TEN

Turcot, Sharon, as told to Cheryl Knight, Ph.D., *Sharon's Stories* (Boone, NC: Appalachian State University), 11.

Lamott, Anne. *Traveling Mercies: Some Thoughts on Faith* (New York, NY: Pantheon Books, 1999), 134.

CHAPTER ELEVEN

Borg, Marcus. *Meeting Jesus Again for the First Time* (San Francisco, CA: Harper, 1994), 55.

Barclay, William. *The Gospel Of John, vol. 1* (Edinburgh, Scotland: The Saint Andrew Press, 1956), xxxi.

CHAPTER TWELVE

Hughes, Robert. "Free Libraries, Free Society," *American Libraries* (August 2002), 50.

CHAPTER THIRTEEN

Gooch, Brad. *God Talk: Travels in Spiritual America* (New York, NY: Knopf, 2002), 72.

Andreas, Joel. *Addicted To War* (Oakland, CA: AK Press, 2002), 41–42.

Taylor, Barbara Brown. *Gospel Medicine* (Boston, MA: Cowley Publications, 1995), 70–71.

Cash, Johnny, with Patrick Carr. *Johnny Cash: The Autobiography* (New York, NY: HarperCollins, 1997), 300.

CHAPTER FOURTEEN

Spoto, Donald. *Reluctant Saint: The Life of St. Francis of Assisi* (New York, NY: Viking Compass, 2002), 212.